D0426062

POCKET
MBA

OTHER TITLES FROM
THE ECONOMIST BOOKS

The Economist Desk Companion
The Economist Economics
The Economist Guide to Economic Indicators
The Economist Guide to the European Union
The Economist Numbers Guide
The Economist Style Guide
The Guide to Analysing Companies
The Guide to Financial Markets
The Guide to Management Ideas
The Dictionary of Economics
The International Dictionary of Finance
Going Digital
Improving Marketing Effectiveness
Management Development
Managing Complexity
Measuring Business Performance

Pocket Accounting
Pocket Advertising
Pocket Director
Pocket Economist
Pocket Finance
Pocket International Business Terms
Pocket Internet
Pocket Investor
Pocket Law
Pocket Manager
Pocket Marketing
Pocket Money
Pocket Negotiator
Pocket Strategy

The Economist Pocket Asia
The Economist Pocket Europe in Figures
The Economist Pocket World in Figures

The Economist Books

POCKET MBA

THE ECONOMIST IN ASSOCIATION WITH
PROFILE BOOKS LTD

Profile Books Ltd
58A Hatton Garden, London EC1N 8LX

First published by
The Economist Books Ltd 1992

Copyright © The Economist Newspaper Ltd, 1992, 1994, 1997, 2000

All rights reserved. Without limiting the rights under copyright reserved above, no part of this publication may be reproduced, stored in or introduced into a retrieval system, or transmitted, in any form or by any means (electronic, mechanical, photocopying, recording or otherwise), without the prior written permission of both the copyright owner and the publisher of this book.

The greatest care has been taken in compiling this book. However, no responsibility can be accepted by the publishers or compilers for the accuracy of the information presented.
Where opinion is expressed it is that of the author and does not necessarily coincide with the editorial views of
The Economist Newspaper.

Typest in Garamond by MacGuru
info@macguru.org.uk

Printed in Italy by
LEGO S.p.a. – Vicenza – Italy

A CIP catalogue record for this book is available
from the British Library

ISBN 1 86197 256 3

Contents

Introduction

Pocket MBA is one in a series of books that brings the clarity for which *The Economist* is famous to the often confusing subject of management.

It is written by Tim Hindle, a former business editor, management editor and finance editor of The Economist, and is divided into three main parts.

Part 1 consists of essays that look at management education, classic management literature, the development of the MBA in the 20th century and its likely role in the 21st century.

Part 2 is an A–Z of management ideas and thinkers, focusing on the main academic disciplines that are taught at business schools. The A–Z stretches from Chris Argyris to Max Weber; and from Frederick Winslow Taylor to Rosabeth Moss Kanter and Peter Senge. It includes entries on *kanban*, Pareto's principle and portfolio theory, among many others.

In this section words in small capitals usually indicate a separate entry, thus enabling readers to find other relevant information (though they should note that abbreviations such as BP are also in small capitals).

Part 3 consists of appendices with addresses of selected business schools, useful background information, a selection of websites and a reading list.

The Pocket Management series is designed to take the mystique out of business jargon in a stimulating and entertaining way. Other titles in the series include:

Pocket Accounting
Pocket Advertising
Pocket Director
Pocket Economist
Pocket Finance
Pocket International Business Terms
Pocket Internet
Pocket Investor
Pocket Law
Pocket Manager
Pocket Marketing
Pocket Money
Pocket Negotiator
Pocket Strategy

Part 1

Essays

MANAGEMENT EDUCATION

If you are thinking of doing an MBA, there are seven questions we suggest you ask before dusting down your satchel.

1 What is an MBA?

The MBA (Master of Business Administration) is a post-graduate, post-experience, academic course in a number of subjects that together can be said to constitute the science of management.

In the Anglo-Saxon world such is the kudos of the MBA that many assume it is the only academic business qualification available. But it is not. In Japan there is plenty of management education, but no MBA. In continental Europe much business education is at the undergraduate level. In many countries, the MBA has no legally recognised status. Even in the MBA-besotted UK and United States there are a large number and variety of undergraduate business courses.

People interested in a business career should think twice about going to university to read medieval Russian literature on the understanding that they will do an MBA at a later stage (the only stage at which they can do one) and that the Russian might be useful for an oil job in Baku. Just as it is (almost) never too late to learn about business and management, so it is almost never too early.

2 Are you a suitable candidate for an MBA?

MBA students, of necessity, are generally of a certain age. Because they are expected to have a first degree and some work experience, they are rarely aged under 24. At American business schools, which revel in disclosing the age profiles of their student population, the median age of MBA entrants is 28. Rarely are more than 10% over the age of 30. In European schools the average age is slightly higher.

MBA students fall roughly into three categories.

- Those wanting to go into business after

working in other areas, such as teaching or the civil service.
- Those seeking a career move from one company to another, or from one function (such as engineering) to another, and a salary hike.
- Those wanting to work in sectors, such as management consultancy, where an MBA is almost essential.

In the past, some MBA courses became "car parks" for the disaffected and the redundant, who were waiting for the economy to perk up or for their true talents to be recognised. The leading business schools are trying to rumble these people before they arrive by insisting that students should have defined goals and some idea of where they are going.

3 What are the entry qualifications?

Apart from a recognised degree and (for foreign-language speakers) tests to show proficiency in the language or languages of the course, the only entrance exam for the best schools in the United States and Europe is the Graduate Management Admission Test (GMAT). (For further details see entry in A–Z.)

The GMAT is administered as a computer-adaptive test (known as GMAT CAT) in hundreds of locations throughout the world. A paper-based GMAT is offered twice a year where the network of computer-based testing sites is not yet available. The GMAT CAT is offered three weeks a month, six days a week, throughout the year at more than 400 computer-based testing centres in North America and selected cities around the world. It is always in English, lasts for about three and a half hours, and includes verbal, quantitative and analytical writing questions. The leading business schools take few students with a GMAT score of under 550, although no score (over 700 is exceptional) guarantees a place.

4 How long will the course last?

The length of time you need to set aside for an MBA depends on the type of course you choose. A full-time, on-campus course – a blue-chip MBA – will take two academic years at most American schools and one year at most European schools.

If you want to, or have to, carry on working while taking your MBA there are numerous part-time courses on offer. Study takes place in the evenings or at weekends, and many programmes require students to gather on campus for a residential week or two each year. Part-time courses take around three years to complete. They have several advantages – for example, they cost less and students can put into practice in their jobs the things they learn as they learn them. Their main disadvantage is that they do not foster the community spirit that many full-time MBA students find so valuable.

Another type of MBA, the modular MBA, has been created specifically for students sponsored by their employers. It aims to tackle two of the criticisms of traditional MBA programmes: that they are too academic and that they lack relevance to real business. Students take modules of a traditional MBA at a business school, but much more of their time is spent on projects with their employer. In some cases, companies or groups of companies offer their own MBAS in conjunction with a business school.

Consortium programmes are a form of modular MBA where several companies and a business school get together to design a course. The aim is to provide the companies involved with a means of developing their employees that takes a broad perspective yet remains clearly relevant to their own business.

Lastly, there are distance-learning programmes, which get around the problem of there being too few good teachers to meet the demand for MBAS. These programmes can be taken at an even more remote distance from a school than the part-time programmes, and they take even longer. Pre-packaged learning materials are sent to students to study at home, and they spend occasional residential weeks and weekends on campus. The Internet has given a boost to distance learning, with the use of e-mail, CD-ROM, computer networks, communication systems (such as Lotus Notes) and videoconferencing. Many schools provide personal tutors, telephone hotlines, summer schools, weekend seminars and local support groups. But beware: distance learning can be a lonely activity.

5 How much will it cost?

Fees vary enormously, depending on the type of programme and the business school chosen. Annual tuition fees alone at some American schools are over $25,000. A one-year course at INSEAD can easily set you back some $45,000 in fees and living costs. On top of this is the opportunity cost of lost earnings while following a full-time MBA programme.

Part-time and distance-learning programmes cost less. Students who are sponsored by their company to do a modular course may find it costs them nothing at all.

Some commercial banks offer special loan schemes to finance MBA studies, and many business schools offer financial aid for potential students, including bursaries, scholarships, assistantships, grants and loans.

6 What sorts of things will you learn?

Most MBA courses contain a common core of subjects that have to be covered. These include:

- business economics;
- strategy;
- human resources;
- marketing;
- finance;
- operations management;
- e-commerce.

Some of the teaching is likely to follow the case-study method pioneered by Harvard Business School.

Different schools offer different optional courses (or electives), usually selected from a wide range of subjects. The subjects offered may vary from year to year, so it is important to get hold of the most up-to-date information. Depending on your special interests, these options can be a crucial factor in determining which school you attend.

All courses require a certain amount of work to be done in teams, as well as independent work on at least one major project with, sometimes, a lengthy dissertation to top it off. The balance between class work and project work differs greatly between schools. Manchester Business School, for example, is very project-oriented; London Business School is fonder of the classroom.

7 Which school is most suitable?

Having considered questions 1–6 it is now time to choose a school. A 1999 survey by the Economist Intelligence Unit found a number of criteria cited by MBA graduates as their reason for choosing one school rather than another. The reputation of the school was the most important, with more respondents outside Europe and North America rating this highly. Programme content came second, with more in Europe and North America rating this highly. Third came location, although this is clearly not particularly relevant for distance learning.

	%
Reputation of school	34
Programme content	19
Location	14
Quality of teaching faculty	10
Published sources	9
Friends' recommendation	4
Teaching methods	4
Careers services record	1
Starting salary of graduates	1

It should not be surprising that the reputation of

the school comes top of the list. MBA graduates increasingly find that having an MBA is not enough in a world where so many people have them. Employers are more interested now in where the MBA is from. This has made the business schools more competitive, and more concerned about the quality of their courses.

If, however, by now you have decided that you cannot cope with an MBA, do not despair. Management education should not be something that is packed into one hectic, expensive ten-month period (or even a 21-month period) early in a manager's career. It should be a continuous process for life that any employer worth working for will be monitoring and encouraging at all times.

Management literature

Modern management literature, it is generally acknowledged, began with the publication in 1911 of Frederick Winslow Taylor's *The Principles of Scientific Management.* Since then there has been a steady stream of writing about the various aspects of running a business. Some of it has undoubtedly exerted a strong influence on management practice, and some of it has contributed to the body of knowledge now known as business or management studies. But the vast majority of it, unfortunately, has done neither. In its attempts to gain for itself some semblance of academic respectability, most management writing has ended up being about as exciting to read as the rules of netball.

The writing has come from three principal sources: academics reporting research or developing theoretical constructs; practitioners of management who write about the lessons of their own experience; and management consultants drawing on their various cases.

Taylor himself falls into the last category. As an efficiency expert, he advocated that managers should gather together all the traditional knowledge possessed by workmen, and should then classify it and reduce it to laws, rules and formulae. They should develop a "science" for each element of a man's work to replace old "rule-of-thumb" methods, and they should "scientifically" select and train workers in the new methods. Lastly, managers should take over certain tasks, such as planning and scheduling, which were previously left to workmen to cope with as best they could.

The early years

Taylor's work had a profound influence on the management of manufacturing industry, and much workshop practice (particularly the use of work study techniques) still reflects this today. There were, however, other writers in the period before the second world war who exercised a similarly strong influence. The most notable were Henri Fayol, a French mining engineer; Elton Mayo, an Australian professor at Harvard; Mary Parker Follett, an American educationalist; Chester Barnard, president of the New Jersey Bell Telephone Company; and Lyndall F. Urwick, a British army officer turned management consultant.

Fayol's work was first published in French in 1916 under the title *Administration Industrielle et Générale*, but it failed to be noticed in the United States and the UK until an English translation appeared in 1949. Since then it has proved enduringly popular. Fayol broke management down into five elements – planning, organising, commanding (or directing), co-ordinating and controlling – a framework adopted by countless others since.

Elton Mayo is widely regarded as the founder of the so-called human-relations school, a group of writers who put special emphasis on the human factor. His best-known work, *The Human Problems of an Industrial Civilisation*, was based on the famous studies he conducted at the Hawthorne works of the Western Electric company in the United States. He believed that human motivation, emotional attitudes to work and social relationships were more important determinants of productivity than logical layouts of the workplace or "scientific" schemes for rationalising work.

Mary Parker Follett reached similar conclusions, but on philosophical grounds rather than by means of research. In *Freedom and Co-ordination* she emphasised the importance of group processes in decision making, and she had much to say that remains relevant today in the context of conflict resolution.

Chester Barnard's analysis of the managerial role and the nature of organisations was an important contribution to managerial sociology. His book *The Functions of the Executive* linked together hitherto unrelated ideas about the factors affecting individual performance, the nature of organisations and managerial processes.

The last person in this group, Lyndall F. Urwick, produced *The Elements of Administration*, a new synthesis based on the ideas of Taylor, Fayol and Follett. His principles have become known as the "classical" principles of management. But they are increasingly criticised as lacking relevance in the modern business environment, perhaps most notably in recent years by Henry Mintzberg. Mintzberg's seminal research on what managers actually do showed them to be ad hoc and reactive, responding minute-by-minute to crises of greater or lesser import. Fayol's five elements, so good in theory, seemed less so in practice.

Post-war writers

The rebuilding of industries after the second world war had a significant impact on management writing. Foremost in the field is Peter Drucker, arguably the 20th century's most influential writer on management. His shrewd analysis of the key changes in the business environment (and their implications for managerial work) combined timeliness and relevance with an unusually attractive literary style.

Drucker has written so many important works that it is difficult to single out which has been the most influential. With hindsight, possibly his most valuable contribution was the *Age of Discontinuity*, written in the late 1960s. It turned out to be a remarkably accurate guide to those changes in the 1970s and 1980s that had a profound impact on business.

Among the practitioners-turned-writers, two of the most influential have been Lee Iacocca of Chrysler and Alfred Sloan of General Motors, both of them (curiously) from the American motor industry. Probably better known outside management circles are the works of a small number of influential authors who have illuminated management thought with humour or satire, notably C. Northcote Parkinson's *Parkinson's Law*, Robert Townsend's *Up the Organisation* and Scott Adams's *The Dilbert Principle*.

Contributions from academics that have

become an accepted part of the body of knowledge have mainly involved the human factor. Books such as Douglas McGregor's *The Human Side of Enterprise*, Abraham Maslow's *Motivation and Personality* and Frederick Herzberg's *The Motivation to Work* remain the best texts on the role of the manager. Charles Handy's bestseller *Understanding Organisations* is probably the most widely read and understood guide to the complex nature of the modern work organisation. Nevertheless, there are many examples of outstanding contributions to the body of management literature by writers from other disciplines.

Two academics, Theodore Levitt and Philip Kotler, have made lasting contributions in the field of marketing, and Michael Porter of Harvard is today's acknowledged master of the central function of business strategy. In the operations area three writers on quality – P.B. Crosby, W. Edwards Deming and J.J. Juran – have achieved international reputations.

Followers of fashion

In the last decades of the 20th century, management literature mirrored the management fashions of the time. In the 1980s the main routes to a bestseller were to write about quality, leadership and/or the art of Japanese management. The bestselling business book of the decade, *In Search of Excellence*, combined elements of all three. Generally regarded as the most influential book on management to date, "Excellence" became almost a cult, establishing large fortunes and a worldwide reputation for its authors, Tom Peters and Bob Waterman.

Two books that came out in the early 1990s set the trend for the rest of that decade. One was Peter Senge's *The Fifth Discipline*, which suggested that all managers should think about their business as a dynamic, ever-changing "system". This led the way for a shelf of books on managing change (with titles like *Think Change!*) and another shelf on the by then moribund art of system dynamics.

The second key book of the 1990s was *Reengineering the Corporation* by Michael Hammer and James Champy, the powerful combination of an academic and a consultant. It coincided with the recession in the United States and the UK in the early years of the decade and provided firms with some intellectual justification for slashing layers and layers of managers in an orgy of "downsizing". The book was important, however, for the way it persuaded companies to focus on processes (a series of business activities) rather than on traditional functions (like "marketing" or "finance"). Business process re-engineering (or BPR) became the thing to do, and the way to do it was through cross-functional teamwork.

By the end of the 20th century, the fashions in management literature were beginning to revolve around e-commerce (in any shape or form) and branding. There were signs also of a vogue for books that reflected the ever-widening interest in spirituality and self-examination. *The New Unblocked Manager* was one *fin de siècle* title (which was not, of course, about drains), and in the early months of the 21st century the Dalai Lama's *Ethics for the New Millennium* found its way on to the list of transcendent business books.

No survey of management literature, however brief, would be complete without a reference to the *Harvard Business Review*. This bi-monthly magazine has long been unrivalled as a means of access to new management thinking and as a source of intellectual stimulation. It is likely to carry on as the arbiter of literary fashion for managers well into the 21st century.

THE MBA IN THE 20TH CENTURY

Over a period of almost 30 years, from the beginning of the 1960s to the end of the 1980s, the MBA was transformed from being the Cinderella of professional qualifications into being the *sine qua non* for every aspiring manager. By the 1990s the MBA had (arguably) become the most sought-after qualification on the planet.

It had, however, had a difficult upbringing. In its earliest years it had had to struggle to gain academic respectability, largely because in the two countries where it was first developed (the United States and the UK) it was fostered within the framework of long-established, non-vocational universities. This meant that the first business courses were nurtured with an eye on the academic values that such universities upheld. These emphasised the importance of pure research, and directed the courses towards academic disciplines that were already recognised, such as statistics, accounting and economics. This bypassed many of the things that businessmen said they wanted to find in the graduates of such courses, such as entrepreneurial initiative, the ability to communicate and leadership. For the most part, it bypassed them because universities did not have the faintest idea how to teach them.

The universities stood uncomfortably between the supply of MBA graduates and the demand for them (from industry and commerce). In general, industry believed that managers were born, not made. The level of management training in most countries was abysmally low. Even in 1985, more than 70% of British managers had received no training for their jobs. Traditional managers thought that the early MBA graduates were arrogant, difficult to fit into established career paths and bloated with high expectations about their worth.

Nevertheless, the number of universities sprouting business schools and MBA courses increased dramatically. In 1965 there were only two MBA courses in the UK (at London and Manchester business schools); today there are over 100. In the United States there were only 5,000 new MBAS being created every year at the beginning of the 1960s; by the end of the 1980s the number had risen to over 70,000 a year.

Something was going right. And it was, at first, the demand from students. Leading American schools found themselves receiving thousands of applications for, at most, a few hundred places. New schools were spawned on the back of the old schools' rejects. Many tried to differentiate themselves by offering specialised MBAS in the fashionable sectors of the 1980s, such as finance or retailing.

The reason for this sudden upsurge in demand has never been satisfactorily explained, but it became a virtuous circle. The brightest undergraduate students were attracted to the courses, and as soon as they had finished they went looking for jobs. Employers then realised that to find the brightest recruits all they had to do was to trawl through the business schools' beauty parades.

The virtuous circle was given a further boost by the emphasis that universities' business faculties placed on finding jobs for their output. Careers services became one of the main factors in the success or otherwise of a business school. The people that ran the services had a tremendous influence on the MBA "industry", in terms of the types of jobs that graduates went into and, to some extent, the design of the MBA programme itself. The criticisms that careers officers brought back from recruiters, especially of the lack of teaching of the soft skills – how to manage people – started a wholesale revamping of MBA programmes in the late 1980s and early 1990s.

Significantly, the Japanese and Germans built successful industrial models that did not include the MBA. This was partly because they had other ways of teaching people how to be managers. In continental Europe undergraduate business education was more widespread than in either the United States or the UK. In Japan there was a sophisticated system in which learning took place largely on the job. This inculcated not only business lessons but also the culture of the employer's organisation, which is such an important element in Japanese management.

The few business schools that did develop in continental Europe grew not from the tertiary educational system, but from the demands of industry. For example, INSEAD, in Fontainebleau, France, was started by a group of businessmen with help from the Paris Chamber of Commerce. IMD, in Lausanne, Switzerland, is the result of a merger between IMI and IMEDE, two Swiss schools started as in-house training centres by a couple of multinational companies, Alcan and Nestlé respectively.

Recession and change

The recession of the early 1990s proved a watershed for the university-based business schools. Job opportunities did not drop into their students' laps with quite the same ease as they had in the 1980s. The powerful careers' offices were forced to become much more active in developing new job opportunities for their graduates and in wooing non-traditional MBA recruiters.

The traditional big recruiters of the time – management consultants and the financial-services industry – suddenly stopped the "bulk buying" of MBA graduates that had powered the boom in the second half of the 1980s. When these industries returned to the market, they did so in a more selective way than previously. The number of American businesses that were recruiting MBA graduates from three or more of the leading American universities fell sharply, to little more than 200. For reasons of economy, time and perceptions of quality, recruiters increasingly chose to restrict their efforts to just a few schools.

This helped to turn the industry into one where the winner takes all. A small number of elite schools were able to become more and more elite, because the brightest students soon realised that the employers they wanted to reach were valuing an MBA graduate from only a small number of highly select schools. This taught all the business schools that what they really needed to do was to address the basics, the things that industry expected of them. The most basic thing, they were being told, was to develop the future senior managers of manufacturing and service industries.

As a consequence, many schools began radically to reassess the nature of their courses, often in close consultation with industry. In the forefront was the University of Pennsylvania's Wharton School, traditionally a training-ground for fast-moving Wall Street financiers. After wide consultation with a number of chief executives and company recruiters, Wharton decided to move away from its traditional number-crunching specialisation in order to create a more general management course. This approach became almost the charter for all business schools in the 1990s.

It is one thing to define what is needed, but quite another to produce it. Teaching the so-called soft skills, such as leadership and negotiation, proved to be no easy task. It was not helped by the fact that the schools were constantly stretched to find academic staff of the right calibre in the old traditional disciplines, not to mention these new soft ones, which industry sometimes thought boiled down to little more than instinct and upbringing.

Then, as the 20th century drew to a close, there were two new subjects to be taught: the Internet and globalisation. Where were the teachers of these to be found, and how would business schools and MBA courses adapt to the challenges of the 21st century?

THE MBA IN THE 21ST CENTURY

The role of the MBA in future is likely to be very different from what it was in the 20th century. In the 1990s it was the acknowledged route to the upper echelons of finance and consulting, the two fields that high-flyers most aspired to. Able young men and women who wanted to shine at Gatsby-style parties in Chelsea or Long Island had to be able to say that they worked for Goldman Sachs or McKinsey, or their equivalents.

Then, like all fads, it faded out of fashion. Two things in particular brought about the change. First, there was a competing fad that appeared suddenly and without much notice. This was the idea, at the heart of the so-called new economy, that any 28-year-old worth his or her business salt should, by that age, be well on the way to their first IPO and their first million-dollar cheque. This hit the consulting firms and the investment banks hard. Many of the brightest MBA graduates, for whom a job offer from the likes of the Boston Consulting Group had for years been a "no brainer", found that they could be enticed by an unknown start-up dangling a package of share options.

As Stan Miranda, the head of worldwide recruiting for the consulting firm Bain & Co, put it at the end of 1999: "I go to Harvard Business School and I sit down with these guys [the MBA students] and all they want to do is talk about their business plans."

The second influence on the MBA students' change of heart was the gradual realisation that when they got the job of their dreams on Wall Street, or with a firm of high-powered strategy consultants, they ended up as little more than number-crunchers. Locked away in a downtown office, they put together the data and the Powerpoint presentations that enabled the firms' partners to impress clients with the depth of their "research". They got a decent salary, but they increasingly saw their savvy friends working in small dot coms with, as Dr Johnson once put it, "the potentiality of growing rich, beyond the dreams of avarice". They wanted to get a bit of that potentiality too.

So the brightest MBA graduates started to go elsewhere. Whereas 38% of the 1995 crop of Harvard MBAS went into consulting, by 1999 the comparable figure was only 29%.

The ethos of the new economy even made some students think again about the fundamental value of an MBA. The new economy emphasised the value to be gained from the softer side of management, from vision and teamwork and suchlike. Young entrepreneurs on the west coast of the United States, the role model for the times, just hung out together in groups and set out to solve problems. Had a highly structured course at a business school anything to offer them?

As Mark McCormack, author of the 1980s bestseller *What They Don't Teach You at Harvard Business School*, once said, "business schools are, of necessity, condemned to teach the past". The case-study approach pioneered by Harvard made that inevitably true. The new economy, however, was fast teaching a whole generation of would-be entrepreneurs that whatever the future would be, it would be nothing like the past. There was no point in learning how to run the IBM of the 1990s when all you wanted to do was to run the Internet-based star of the 2000s.

This fad too, of course, had its span. Some of the consultancy defectors received an early shock. For example, one of the high-profile first generation of dot com companies was a London-based online clothing retailer called boo.com. It managed to lure no fewer than 22 consultants from their cosy nests to work for it in the months before it went online in November 1999. Six months later, however, both the consultants' share options and their jobs went pear-shaped when boo.com failed to find any more financiers to feed it.

In the meantime, the consulting firms had felt the pinch and began to talk about a "War for Talent". In an article with this title in the *McKinsey*

Quarterly in autumn 1998, the authors wrote, "Ten years ago McKinsey's new hires were almost all MBAS; now over 40% are lawyers, doctors, economists, scientists, military officers or former government officials."

Other traditional MBA recruiters also widened the trawl in their search for talent. McKinsey quoted the cases of an American accounting firm, which hired one-third of one year's graduates from a leading Indian college, and Enron, a fast-growing utility, which recruited retired military officers because "people from the army are used to travelling a lot, and this work is like what they have been doing".

This highlights a key ingredient that employers are increasingly looking for: skills that can be transported. The enduring growth of globalisation has put a premium on people who can work in a variety of cultural and commercial environments. Firms try more and more to recruit locally and to avoid sending their employees abroad in the style of the traditional expatriates who manned the first wave of internationalisation. This is partly because of the cost, and partly because employees are less prepared to accept the disruption it causes to their children's education and to their partners' careers. Nevertheless, it is a structure that demands more and more interaction with other cultures, both inside and outside an organisation.

The business schools have not been slow to latch on to this need. They too have sought to make their MBA courses more international. In this the European schools have stolen a march on the traditional American market leaders. European employers value the output of institutions such as INSEAD and London Business School more highly than they do that of Wharton or Stanford. Increasingly, too, they like schools where the teaching is in more than one language.

At the beginning of 2000, INSEAD took the brave step of opening an entirely new campus in Singapore. Some 55 students enrolled on its one-year MBA programme and eight of its faculty moved permanently from Fontainebleau to the South-East

Asian island state. The school's dean, Antonio Borges, said at the time of the opening, "There's a greater need for international managers than ever before."

Some schools thought that the combined technologies of the Internet and videoconferencing would, before long, pre-empt such an expensive move. Long-promised distance learning would, they thought, soon come into its own for the MBA. But even some of the more conservative American schools began to put their toes (albeit more modestly than INSEAD) into foreign waters. Northwestern University's highly respected Kellogg Graduate School of Management joined up with the University of Pennsylvania's Wharton School to support a new Indian School of Business (the ISB), located just outside Hyderabad. Kellogg and Wharton intend to oversee the ISB's MBA curriculum – the first students are scheduled to arrive in 2001 – and they will send staff there to teach on temporary assignments. The new school's students will also be able to sit in (via satellite) on lectures being delivered at the two American institutions.

The driving force behind the ISB was Rajat Gupta, a Calcutta-born senior partner at McKinsey. No doubt his firm will be an enthusiastic hirer of the ISB's graduates when they appear. Or will those graduates just want to start a dot com down the road, the location of India's very own burgeoning Silicon Valley?

Part 2

A–Z

ABC

Short for Activity-Based Costing, a system of assigning costs to products and services within a business according to the resources that they consume. At heart, ABC is a means to escape from the traditional way of allocating indirect costs in proportion to direct costs, and from the limitations of such a method. ABC allocates indirect costs according to the amount of resources (lighting, MARKETING, R&D, for example) actually consumed by each specific product. In particular, this increases the relative cost of highly customised products.

Accounting principles

In the United States, accounting principles are the umpteen detailed accounting rules that the profession agrees to follow. What Americans call accounting principles, however, the British refer to as accounting practices.

Accounting principles in the UK are something more fundamental, and can be roughly divided into four.

- The going concern principle. Always assume that the company whose accounts you are preparing is a going concern, or at least that it will be until you next come to look at its accounts.
- The principle of prudence. If in doubt, be prudent.
- The matching principle. Revenue and expenses should be recorded in the period when they arise, not in the period when they are actually received or paid.
- The principle of consistency. If in doubt, do what you did last time.

But these principles can clash. For example, GOODWILL is paid for when another company is bought, but the revenue from it accrues over a number of years. So the matching principle says that the expense of goodwill should be spread over several years' accounts. Yet prudence whispers that there may never be any revenue to match the goodwill expense, in which case the expense should appear in the accounts of the period when it was paid.

As clever accountants have continually shown, you can create widely differing pictures of a company's financial strength according to the accounting principles that you adopt.

Accounting standards

When accountants are uncertain about how to VALUE particular items in a company's accounts, their professional associations get together to rule on what they consider to be BEST PRACTICE. This advice is then issued in the form of an accounting standard which, when applied, makes it easier to compare the financial performance of one company with that of another. Some say that such standards succeed in making all accounts pear-shaped, just so that readers of the accounts can compare pears with pears and not with apples.

Particularly controversial areas that the associations have tried to rule on include accounting for inflation, for foreign-currency conversion, for deferred tax and for GOODWILL.

Different countries give their standards different weight. In Canada they have legal backing. In the United States they are compulsory for companies registered with the Securities and Exchange Commission. But in the UK they are voluntary, although any company not complying with them has to explain why.

Acquisition cost

The cost of a corporate acquisition, like the cost of a house, is higher than the purchase price. First you have to add on the fees of the bankers, the lawyers and the accountants that have inevitably been involved in the deal; then comes the cost of changing the workforce (redundancy pay), or the plant and machinery, in order to improve the business. When the full cost of an acquisition is calculated, it is enough to raise doubts in the minds of all but the most ardent acquirers.

ADDED VALUE
Or value added, the difference between what a company spends in buying materials from outside, and what it receives from selling its products or services. Out of this so-called added value the firm has to pay wages, rent and interest. The rest is PROFIT.

Calculating the added value at different stages of a production PROCESS can help a company to identify the most profitable parts of its business. The calculation may throw up the fact that certain processes can be bought more cheaply from outside and should, therefore, be OUTSOURCED.

ADVERTISING
The use of media (newspapers, television, and so on) to inform consumers about a product or service and to try to persuade them to buy it. Advertising is an important part of MARKETING, but not (as many advertising agencies would have it) the sum total of it.

Advertising is not solely concerned with the selling of commercial products. In most industrialised countries, the producers of goods and services account for about half of all advertising expenditure. The other half comes from intermediaries (such as retailers), governments, non-government agencies (such as charities), and from individuals (often in the form of classified advertising). (See also TEASER.)

AGENT
A company or individual who has the authority to carry out transactions with third parties on behalf of somebody else (who is called the principal). Agents are frequently used to buy or sell goods in remote or inaccessible markets. There are two main types.

- A sole agent is an agent with an exclusive agreement to be the only person (or company) allowed to buy or sell on behalf of the principal in a particular geographic region.

- A commission agent is someone who is rewarded by a commission; that is, an agreed percentage of the VALUE of the goods that he or she buys or sells.

In one sense, managers are the agents of a company's shareholders. Some have seen the shortcomings of this agency relationship as one of the central failings of capitalism.

ALLIANCE

The joining together of two corporations (which can sometimes be rivals) in a loose link for what they see as being their mutual benefit. Alliances can take many different forms, ranging from a JOINT VENTURE to a FRANCHISE agreement or a LICENSING arrangement. The term is not generally used to refer to acquisitions or PREFERRED SUPPLIERS.

Alliances are being used increasingly by companies as a strategic route to growth. They are less expensive than one alternative (acquisitions) and quicker than another (internal growth). In recent years, large corporations have formed literally hundreds of strategic alliances with different partners around the world. Managing this NETWORK of loose associations is a key task for managers.

ALUMNI

Most business schools have associations of former students (alumni) that they foster with varying degrees of enthusiasm. These associations can be helpful to the schools in creating job opportunities or work experience for their current crop of students, and as a starting point for any fundraising activity. They can also be useful to former students as a NETWORK of lifelong business contacts.

ANDERSEN CONSULTING

The world's largest management consulting firm and a leader in the IT consulting business. Since 1989 it has been a unit of Andersen Worldwide, a PARTNERSHIP that is the umbrella organisation for it and for Arthur Andersen, the original accountancy firm from which grew the consulting business.

The neat division between accounting and consulting has become blurred in recent years as Arthur Andersen has increasingly entered the consulting business in its own name. This has led Andersen Consulting to seek a complete split from what was once its other half.

All new recruits to the firm go through Andersen's famous three-week course at its "campus" at St Charles, near Chicago.

IGOR ANSOFF

Like a remarkably large number of leading American management gurus, Igor Ansoff was born outside the United States (in his case in Vladivostok). He came to the country comparatively late in life (at the age of 16) and worked for Lockheed for some years before pursuing an academic career that quickly focused on corporate STRATEGY.

Ansoff was one of the first people to emphasise the importance of the external environment in the shaping of corporate strategy. Hitherto, strategy had been heavily influenced by the internal needs of the corporation: continuing employment, utilisation of resources, and the whims and desires of senior managers.

Over the years, Ansoff moved from rather rigid prescriptions for planning procedures to less quantifiable recipes for effecting change in a turbulent environment.

I would like to be recognised as one of the first to offer a scientific proof that the age of universal prescriptions (such as "stick to your knitting") is over; that the solution depends on the characteristics of the organisation's environment; that each organisation needs to diagnose its future environment and then devise its own appropriate solutions.

Igor Ansoff

ANTITRUST LAWS

American legislation, first passed in 1890, which makes it illegal to set up monopolies that are harmful to competition. The legislation also makes it illegal to act in restraint of trade, by operating a CARTEL, for example.

The antitrust laws have been a powerful weapon against industrial CONCENTRATION in the United States and against the exploitation of monopolies. One of the first companies to become a victim of the legislation was National Cash Register (NCR), which in 1912 was successfully prosecuted for its aggressive MARKETING tactics.

The European Union and many other countries operate strict antitrust laws to combat monopolies and cartels.

APPRAISAL

A formal procedure to assess the performance of an employee during a given period, usually a year. At their annual appraisal, employees can expect not only to discuss their performance during the preceding 12 months but also to consider their development and training needs over the next year.

ARBITRAGE

Buying a commodity or currency in one market in order to sell it almost immediately in another, and to make a PROFIT from the price differences between the two. In effect, arbitrage smoothes out imperfections between different parts of a market.

Whenever arbitrage takes place, it reduces the opportunity for further arbitrage. Suppose there is an inconsistency in the exchange rates of the yen, the Swiss franc and the dollar. Somebody makes a profit by selling yen for Swiss francs in Tokyo, using the francs to buy dollars in Geneva, before selling the dollars for yen in New York. (Such a person will, of course, have to buy and sell in large quantities to ensure that the dealing charges on the transactions do not eat up all the profit.) Such arbitrage transactions naturally smooth out the inconsistencies that gave rise to them in the first place.

In the 1980s the word was extended to refer to dealings in stocks and shares, where it was sometimes referred to as risk arbitrage. Arbitrageurs (commonly known as arbs) were people who bought the shares of companies that they suspected were about to be subject to a TAKEOVER bid (or bought the right to buy such shares at an agreed price in the future). Since a bid would automatically push up the price of these shares, arbs could subsequently sell them at a profit.

ARBITRATION

An alternative procedure to the courts for settling commercial disputes. Those in dispute (over, say, the terms of a contract) turn to an independent third party whose judgment they have agreed, in advance, to accept should a dispute arise. The third party (the arbitrator) may be a panel of experts, one of whom has been appointed to make the final decision. An arbitrator's judgment is known as an award.

Several international bodies (including some international industry associations) have set up arbitration systems to help settle international commercial disputes.

Arbitration has a number of advantages.

- It is usually cheaper and quicker than going through the courts.
- The parties to the dispute can choose as arbitrator someone who knows their own specialist business.
- The process can take place in secret.
- The venue and timing of the process is much more flexible.
- Even when committed to arbitration, the parties involved do not necessarily give up their right subsequently to take their case to court.

CHRIS ARGYRIS

One of the most influential behavioural psychologists to have worked in the field of management. A professor at Harvard Business School, Argyris wrote a string of books beginning with his classic, *Personality and Organisation*, published in 1957.

His consistent theme was the interweaving of the needs and abilities of the individual with those of the organisation. With Donald Schon, he developed the idea of DOUBLE-LOOP LEARNING. He also anticipated the management thinkers of today who question the blind corporate search for growth, seemingly for its own sake.

ASSEMBLY LINE

A revolutionary system of manufacturing (for its time) in which the product comes to the worker, instead of the worker coming to the product. An article moves along a line of workers, each of whom (called a station) adds a bit of assembly before the article passes on to the next worker. Ultimately, the finished product drops off the end of the line.

One problem with assembly-line production is that unless each station's task takes exactly the same amount of time, the PROCESS is inefficient. Workers can be left idle while a process is being completed further up the line.

ASSETS

Items that are expected to produce economic benefits in the future; the opposite of LIABILITIES. A more precise definition of such a widely used word has been hard to find. The American accounting profession's definition is "something which brings probable future economic benefits, obtained or controlled by a particular entity, as a result of a past transaction or events" – not exactly blinding in its lucidity.

The definition embraces lots of things that are obviously assets – property, machinery, bank deposits, and so on – things that accountants have no problem in measuring in monetary terms and plonking on a BALANCE SHEET. But the American definition also covers other things that accountants have great difficulty in measuring, and that few companies put in their accounts. These include assets such as well-trained staff, loyal customers, a famous BRAND name, or a charismatic chief executive with a long-term contract.

AUDIT

An independent examination of the financial statements of an organisation, and an opinion as to whether they present a TRUE AND FAIR view of the organisation's state of affairs. Almost everywhere in the world companies are required to be inspected and checked by an outside independent firm of recognised accountants, or by a special government body set up for the purpose.

Auditing is an old business; the word is derived from the Latin for hearing. In olden days it referred to the "hearing" that the owner of land gave to his manager, in which the manager had to account for his stewardship.

In recent years the word has taken on a wider meaning. Companies have internal audits, that is, inspections of the accounts carried out by a committee or individual from inside the business. They also have ENVIRONMENTAL AUDITS, to check that the company is complying with environmental legislation, and social audits, to check that it is doing likewise for social legislation (employee welfare requirements, for example).

AVERAGE COST

Perhaps the most logical way to VALUE stocks (INVENTORY) for the purposes of finding out the full cost of manufacturing an individual item. Average cost is the total cost of manufacturing all of the inventory held by a company, divided by the number of units held.

In practice, accountants prefer to value stocks on the FIFO or LIFO principle. This is partly because average cost has to be complicatedly recalculated every time that a unit is added or taken away from the inventory. But it is also because both FIFO and LIFO give real costs, costs that have actually been incurred for particular units of inventory.

B2B

Shorthand for the business-to-business part of E-COMMERCE – the selling, for example, of car parts to car manufacturers over the INTERNET. Despite the wide publicity gained by B2C, the size of the business-to-business electronic market is vastly greater, as much as ten times greater on some calculations.

B2C

Shorthand for the business-to-consumer part of E-COMMERCE – the selling of goods and services directly to consumers via the INTERNET. The volume of B2C has not grown as rapidly as many pundits predicted, and nowhere near as rapidly as B2B.

Bad debt

Debts come in three standard shapes and an infinite number of sizes. The three shapes are:

- good – where there is no reason to believe that the debt will not be repaid on time;
- doubtful – where it looks as if the debt might not be repaid;
- bad – where the debt appears to be irrecoverable, or where it will cost more to recover it than it is worth (literally).

All debts are born good. Some then become doubtful; of these (it is hoped) only a few become bad. Bad debts can be seen as the price paid by all businesses for the benefit of LIMITED LIABILITY.

Good debts appear as an ASSET on a company's BALANCE SHEET. If the company needs the cash represented by the debts in a hurry it can factor them to a finance business. Firms offering a FACTORING service buy the debts at a discount from the creditor.

As debts change their shape, so their treatment in the creditor's accounts changes. Provisions (a percentage of the total VALUE of the debts) have to be set aside out of PROFITS against those debts that become doubtful. The creditor then has to make a judgment as to whether to pursue the debt through the courts (and risk bankrupting the debtor and getting nothing), or whether to be patient in the hope that the debtor will eventually pay in full.

Bad debts have to be written off in the accounts as a loss; in other words the whole amount has to be deducted from profits.

Balance sheet

A financial statement of the VALUE of a company's ASSETS and LIABILITIES. The balance sheet and the PROFIT AND LOSS ACCOUNT are the backbone of a company's annual report, the yearly account of themselves made by the managers of a company to its owners.

The balance sheet is a snapshot of the worth of a company at the close of play on one particular day. It is a blurred snapshot, however, for several reasons. Some assets cannot be valued by accountants, so they do not appear on the balance sheet (the value of a BRAND, for instance). Others that do appear can be tarted up for the day (see WINDOW DRESSING). But like other things that are tarted up, they can look very different the morning after.

Balanced scorecard

A concept developed by Robert Kaplan, an American professor of accounting, as a means of measuring business performance. Its aim was to overcome the shortcomings of the financial accounts that are the sole source of information about most companies' performance. Kaplan claims that the balanced scorecard is a management system that can "channel energies, abilities and specific knowledge held by people throughout the organisation toward achieving long-term strategic goals". It looks at a business from four main perspectives.

- Customers: how do they see the company?
- Internal: what must the company itself aim to excel at?
- Innovation and learning: can the company continue to improve and to create VALUE?

- Financial: how does the company look to its shareholders?

Barrier to entry
An obstacle that hinders a company from entering a particular market. Such obstacles can occur naturally; for example, only one firm can get the best site for selling a particular product. A hypermarket may pay a high price for a field near a new motorway junction as much to prevent rivals from getting it as to make use of it for itself. Other natural barriers arise because established firms benefit from ECONOMIES OF SCALE that newcomers cannot hope to reap immediately. Newcomers also have to overcome customer LOYALTY to well-established firms in the market.

Artificial barriers to entry can be erected by existing firms in a market to discourage new competition. For example, MARKET LEADERS are able to cut prices (maybe even below cost for a time) to make a newcomer's entry that much more difficult.

Barriers to entry are closely watched by ANTITRUST authorities. In most cases they are perfectly legitimate competitive behaviour, but in the extreme they can constitute what is known as "an abuse of a dominant position".

Barrier to exit
An obstacle discouraging a firm from getting out of a market in which it is making little or no PROFIT. In some cases one firm's BARRIER TO ENTRY can be another firm's barrier to exit. If a firm has increased its production and ADVERTISING in order to raise the hurdle that a new market entrant has to climb, then these same (expensive) things may well discourage that firm from getting out of the market should its competitive STRATEGY not pay off.

Past costs that have to be written off can act as a barrier to exit. So too can future costs yet to be incurred. For example, onerous compensation may have to be paid to get out of long-term contractual obligations, and redundancy payments for unwanted workers can be expensive.

Last, and by no means least, there is the fear of being seen to fail, the factor that more than any other keeps companies in business long after fire alarms have told them to run for the exit.

BATCH

A form of production lying somewhere between the non-stop MASS PRODUCTION of the ASSEMBLY LINE and the artisan manufacture of individual, hand-made items. Batch production fails to glean the advantages of mass production (such as ECONOMIES OF SCALE) and needs to be costed in a special way.

BCG

See BOSTON CONSULTING GROUP.

BELLWETHER

A share, a company, or even an industry that acts as an indicator of general market trends. In most national bond markets, for example, there is a bellwether bond (usually a long-term Treasury issue) that serves as an indicator of the whole market.

Benchmarking is the continuous process of measuring your products, practices and services against your toughest competitors and industry leaders – then continuously improving to close the gap.

David Kearns, when CEO of Xerox Corporation

BENCHMARKING

The practice of studying methods and systems in one company and comparing them with methods and systems in another. Companies usually benchmark themselves against the best-performing companies in their industry or sector. To avoid revealing secrets to corporate rivals, benchmarking is usually carried out by independent third parties. They pool the results from all firms in the market and then publish them as the average of each quarter of the sample (from the best-performing quarter to the worst performing).

Individual firms are then able to place their own performance (which they know) in the context of the industry as a whole.

WARREN BENNIS
A pundit on leadership who worked as an academic in Switzerland, France and the United States. For the most part, Bennis avoided the temptation to distil the essence of leadership into five "golden nuggets", but he did admit to identifying four common skills among those leaders that he studied in detail. He called these: vision, the ability to communicate, trust and the capacity for self-learning. His most famous aphorism is: "Managers do things right; leaders do the right thing."

Fond of literature, Bennis liked to quote Tolstoy's comments on family life: "All happy families resemble each other, while each unhappy family is unhappy in its own way." For "family" read "company".

BEST PRACTICE
The standard within a firm by which other units are judged. For example, a retailer with a chain of shops might decide that one of the shops is a role model for the others to follow. The practices of that shop (such as customer service, stock control, or accounting) are then deemed to be the standard that others should aspire to.

BOARD
The committee of DIRECTORS officially appointed by the shareholders of a company to look after their interests. Many boards are called upon to do little more than meet once a month in the boardroom and then enjoy a good lunch. Keeping the board minutes (the record of the meeting) is one of the most important parts of the ritual of these monthly gatherings.

Boards are often criticised for being self-perpetuating oligarchies, selecting new directors from among their own close acquaintances. Shareholders have the right to reject the board's recommendations, but they rarely exercise this right.

Countries such as Germany and Sweden have two-tier boards: a management board made up of executive directors who direct the company's day-to-day business; and a supervisory board, made up of non-executives who supervise the management board. The most striking difference between this board structure and the Anglo-Saxon structure is not so much its duality as the fact that company workers, or their representatives, sit on management boards.

Boards produce their own political correctness to conceal their dominance: high fees become "compensation", "rewards" or "remuneration"; firing becomes "letting people go", "restructuring", "downsizing" or "rightsizing" ... Directors, like most human beings, protect their own interests and fortify their power.

Anthony Sampson, *Company Man*

BOOK VALUE

The amount at which an item is recorded in the accounts (the books). Items are usually recorded at the lower of cost or net realisable VALUE, but you need look no further than the market for property in central London to realise how absurd and detached from reality this can be.

To be successful in this business, we must have the active desire to be helpful to someone else.

James L. Allen

Any task which can be performed can be measured.

Ed Booz

BOOZ-ALLEN & HAMILTON

One of the oldest firms of MANAGEMENT CONSULTANTS. Booz-Allen & Hamilton started life as a market research company in Chicago in 1914. It grew rapidly in the second world war when it worked for the American navy on improving weapon production systems. It is now a major STRATEGY consultancy, measuring itself against the MARKET LEADER, MCKINSEY.

Boston Consulting Group

A leading firm of strategy consultants founded over 30 years ago by Bruce Henderson, a man who was, like many leading consultants, an engineer by training. The Boston Consulting Group's most famous invention was the GROWTH SHARE MATRIX. With its CASH COWS, dogs and question marks, it was one of the most catchy frameworks ever designed for strategic thinking. Like many catchy ideas, however, it has been accused of being over-simplistic, and even misleading.

BCG (as it is commonly known) provides a vivid example of the way in which firms of management consultants grow out of each other. Bruce Henderson left the Arthur D. Little consultancy to set up the Boston Consulting Group, and one of his firm's early partners was a man called Bill Bain. Bain, in turn, left BCG in the 1970s to set up his own consultancy, Bain & Company, well known for its results-oriented approach to the business.

Darwin is probably a better guide to business competition than economists are.

Bruce Henderson, Boston Consulting Group

BPR

See BUSINESS PROCESS RE-ENGINEERING.

Brainstorming

A style of meeting in which a number of people get together in an unstructured attempt to come up with new ideas or new solutions to problems. The first aim is to generate as many ideas as possible; only later (or maybe even at a different session) are the ideas evaluated.

The original belief was that brainstorming was a more effective way of finding new ways forward than relying on a bunch of individuals working alone. There is some evidence, however, that individuals come up with ideas that are more original, but that they produce fewer of them.

BRAND
The combination of factors that gives one particular product or service its identity and thereby differentiates it from its competitors. It is the essence of the product, the only part of it that its owner cannot OUTSOURCE to others. These factors may be tangible, like a more bouncy sole on a shoe, or they may be intangible, like the aura that ADVERTISING gives to a particular deodorant compared with its virtually identical competitors. The VALUE of a powerful brand can be enormous; some have put a tag of $50 billion on the Coca-Cola brand, for example.

If this business were to be split up, I would be glad to take the brands, trademarks and goodwill. You could have all the bricks and mortar, and I would fare better than you.

John Stuart, when chairman of the Quaker food group

BRAND LOYALTY
The extent to which consumers stay loyal to one BRAND because it satisfies their needs, one of the most important of which is that the values for which it stands fit the values of the consumer. Levi's jeans lost their competitive edge when they failed to shift sufficiently as the values of their loyal 1980s consumers changed in the 1990s.

Each time Virgin entered a new business all the conventional pundits whined that we were stretching the brand too far. Rather than worrying too much about brands being stretched too far, people will have to stretch their imaginations further.

Richard Branson

BRAND STRETCHING
The ability of a company to stretch a successful

BRAND name across a number of products and/or services. One of the most famous instances of brand stretching was the introduction of an ice-cream called Mars, a brand name that had previously been uniquely associated with a chocolate bar. Richard Branson's Virgin brand is also notorious for being stretched.

BREAK-EVEN ANALYSIS

A method of establishing what level of sales is required for a new product to break even – for its revenue to match (or exceed) its costs. The key calculation is to find out how much must be sold in order to cover the fixed costs of the product (interest on money borrowed to buy plant and machinery, ADVERTISING, and so on). Computers have greatly assisted companies to carry out this sort of analysis. The fundamental relationships between revenue, price, and variable and fixed costs can be modelled. Giving different values to the variables can show, for example, which price gives maximum profitability.

BREAK-UP VALUE

The VALUE of a business were it to be broken up – the sum of the prices fetched for all its ASSETS were they to be sold separately. This is very different from the value of the assets sold together as a GOING CONCERN.

The history of modern business is scattered with examples of companies taken over by people (often called asset strippers) who made the simple calculation that the parts of the company were worth more separately than they were as a whole. Once in control of the whole these people proceed to make big profits by selling off the bits.

The break-up value of an individual asset (a car, say) is the value of all its bits and pieces (the plastic, electronics, scrap metal, and so on) sold separately.

BUDGETING

If proof were needed that business and family life

are not far apart, then it lies in the obsession of both with budgeting. Budgeting is the way in which the inevitable financial constraints that exist on both families and managers are brought to bear on STRATEGY. It is the process of allocating a company's capital between competing divisions and investment proposals. Traditionally, this has been done by choosing those investments that seem likely to give the highest (discounted) RATE OF RETURN.

One of the main dangers of budgeting is ossification; last year's budget is simply reproduced this year, with 5% or 10% added on. The family budgeted to take the children to the seaside for two weeks last year. So it does the same for this year. But it forgot that the children are now well into their teens and fed up with buckets and spades. They want to spend a week in London or New York with their friends (and without their parents), an entirely different financial proposition. The same is true in a less blatant way for managers, and the products or BRANDS for which they are responsible. This problem led to the development of ZERO-BASE BUDGETING.

BUSINESS CYCLE

Economic growth is not a smooth uninterrupted process; it goes in cycles. These cycles vary in length, with at least one Russian economist (Nikolai Kondratieff) delineating a background of long cycles of some 50–60 years against which shorter ups and downs are set. Clement Juglar, a Frenchman who first spotted these shorter business cycles in the 1860s, concluded (on the basis of evidence from his native France, and from the UK and the United States) that the cycle averaged 8–10 years. He argued that it was an inevitable consequence of capitalism.

The nature of the business cycle can best be seen by considering a single industry, say shipping. When trade grows, shipping companies increase their freight charges because there is more demand for the space on their ships. The increase in freight charges then persuades the shippers to have more ships built to meet the extra demand. But it takes a long time to build a ship, and by the time one is in the water so are those of competitors who have thought in exactly the same way. So freight prices fall back, and so does the number of shippers prepared to order new ships.

The clever company is the one that spots a business cycle in its earliest stages and then invests rapidly. Not only does this make it ready to reap the benefit at the peak of the cycle, but a forceful early move might also pre-empt rivals who are considering the same STRATEGY.

BUSINESS ETHICS

The body of principles and behaviour that are morally acceptable to business. A series of corporate scandals in the later years of the 20th century brought business ethics out of the closet. Most BUSINESS SCHOOLS now include ethics on their curriculum.

Business ethics usually involves itself in areas such as ADVERTISING and the treatment of individuals at work (sexual harassment, discrimination, and so on) as well as the payment of bribes. Business ethics also makes it plain that actions are not always acceptable simply because they are legal.

Salomon Brothers, a securities firm that was badly affected in the early 1990s by a scandal in which it attempted to rig the US government bond market, subsequently published a two-page advertisement in which its chairman described a test that the company had devised to guide its employees along the morally straight and narrow:

> *Contemplating any business act, an employee should ask himself whether he would be willing to see it immediately described by an informed and critical reporter on the front page of his local paper, there to be read by his spouse, children and friends. At Salomon we simply want no part of any activities that pass legal tests but that we, as citizens, would find offensive.*

Business plan

One of the first steps in starting any new business venture is the preparation of a business plan, a document that sets out in words and figures a projection of how the new business (or the expansion of an old business) is going to proceed. Without a business plan, no budding ENTREPRENEUR or ambitious executive will get through a bank manager's door or into a finance DIRECTOR's office.

Typically, a business plan will contain a one-year detailed projection of activity and a broader projection for the next 3–5 years. There is no prescribed format, but a plan needs (at least) to contain information about: the proposed staff; the product or service to be offered; the premises and equipment from which it is to be produced; and the financial details, including a carefully considered CASHFLOW forecast and a projection of future PROFITS and losses. The plan should be neatly presented, and should start with a short summary of the whole proposal.

A business plan has three main purposes.

- To give the planners a way of clarifying their thoughts by compelling them to put them on paper.
- To persuade bankers or investors to put money into the venture.
- To provide checks along the way, as and when the project is up and running.

Planning is everything. The plan is nothing.
General Dwight D. Eisenhower

Business process re-engineering

An idea that became a fad in the early 1990s, described by its authors, Michael Hammer and James Champy, in their book *Re-engineering the Corporation*, as the "radical redesign of business processes to achieve dramatic improvements in performance". Hammer and Champy placed particular emphasis on three of these words.

- Radical. Firms should go back to the root of every single business PROCESS rather than merely attempt to improve what already existed.
- Processes. Re-engineering inevitably meant redesigning the whole corporation so that it focused on processes and not (as almost all of them had done previously) on functions (such as MARKETING and production).
- Dramatic. The search must be for quantum leaps, not just for incremental improvements on what had gone before.

Business school

There are three types: those offering undergraduate business courses; those offering postgraduate qualifications; and those offering post-experience education and training. Many universities provide all three.

Undergraduate courses generally last for 3–4 years and are often a combination of business studies and something else, such as a language or engineering. Students on the courses have rarely had any experience of business.

The major postgraduate qualification on offer is the MBA. Courses usually run for two academic years (21 calendar months) in the United States and for one year in Europe. Students are expected to have had some business experience.

Post-experience education and training courses rarely last for more than a week or two, the most time that busy senior managers are believed to be able to afford. However, some of the most prestigious courses (such as Harvard's Advanced Management Program and Stanford's Executive Program) last longer.

The idea that management can be learnt in a classroom is fairly new. But it is an idea that has spread fast, and there are now hundreds of business schools throughout the United States and Europe (although, perhaps significantly, there are few in Asia). These schools teach both full-time students (typically on a one- or two-year MBA course) and real-life executives, who attend the schools' short courses and part-time classes.

Business schools ... have perpetuated the notion that a manager with net present value calculations in one hand and portfolio planning in the other can manage any business anywhere.
Gary Hamel and C.K. Prahalad

BUYER'S MARKET
Any market in which supply exceeds demand. Such a market can arise either because the supply of a product has been increased (possibly by the arrival of new entrants in the market), or because the demand for the product has declined (owing to recession, perhaps, or changing consumer tastes).

BY-PRODUCT
Something sellable that is produced as an incidental side-effect of the manufacture of a main product; sawdust by a carpenter, for example. In one sense, the whole of the natural gas industry is nothing more than a by-product of the oil business. By-products used to be considered rather inferior things, but they have recently been changing their image. Industry is increasingly looking to them to help recycle waste from its main manufacturing processes.

By-product DIVERSIFICATION is the creation of a separate business from a by-product of a firm's main business. One example is GMAC, a vast financial services business that grew out of General Motors' need to provide its customers with credit facilities when they buy its cars. Many companies are considering by-product diversification, where their initial set-up costs are low. Airlines have spun off catering businesses, oil refiners have diversified into environmental consultancy, and retailers have followed GM's example and developed financial-services arms.

Call centre

A place where a company gathers a number of employees to handle telephone enquiries and/or to take orders for goods and services provided either by the company itself or by others. A number of changes have led to a steep increase in the number of call centres in recent years, including the growing sophistication of telecommunications services; the decline in call charges following widespread DEREGULATION; and the almost universal access of consumers to a telephone.

Cannibalise

To market a new product or service that knowingly eats into the market of another product or service produced by the same company. When Heinz introduces tinned spaghetti in the shape of letters of the alphabet it knows that it will reduce the sales of its main line of ordinary tinned spaghetti.

The reasons for cannibalising a product may be strategically sound: to meet new competition for the children's share of the tinned spaghetti market, for example, or to deter such competition from entering the market. But the cannibaliser takes the risk of destroying the product that is being cannibalised. If children are the whole market for tinned spaghetti then they may stop buying the ordinary variety altogether.

Capacity

The quantity of goods that a factory or machine can produce within a certain period of time. Managers have devised a number of different concepts of capacity.

- The ideal or maximum capacity is the level of activity that would be attained if circumstances were ideal. This is sometimes called the full capacity.
- Practical capacity is the level at which it is reasonable to expect the factory to operate, given the time lost for repairs to equipment, holidays, and so on.

- Normal capacity is the average level of production needed just to fulfil existing demand for the company's output.
- Excess capacity is the amount of extra volume that a company could produce if all its existing plant and equipment were fully used for 24 hours a day every day. More recently, the expression has been applied to softer ASSETS that are under-utilised, such as BRAND names and management systems.

CAPITAL RECONSTRUCTION
A reorganisation of a company's capital, either to reduce the debt burden at a time when the company is making heavy demands on its CASH-FLOW, or to make use of spare cash in the bank to buy back some of its own shares.

CAPTIVE MARKET
A group of consumers who have no choice as to what products they buy in a particular market. They may be captive because the products are supplied by a monopoly supplier, or they may be captive because they are in a particular situation in which they are denied choice. During a flight, for example, airline travellers can have only the food or drink that the transport company decides to make available to them.

CAREW'S AXE
A phenomenon observed when companies lay off a large number of employees. Those laid off are not those who are least good at their work. Rather, they are those whom it is easiest to get rid of. Or those who can most easily find work elsewhere.

CARTEL
A group of firms in the same line of business that collude in setting prices. The most famous cartel in recent history was the Organisation of Petroleum Exporting Countries (OPEC). Because of its control over the world's oil supplies it was able to fix the price of oil more or less at whatever

level it wished. Its power, however, has waned in recent years, for at least three reasons.

- Oil consumers have found oil in places outside OPEC that are not bound by its price rules.
- OPEC's cartel has encouraged consumers to develop and use alternative forms of fuel.
- It has proved hard at times to keep all members of the cartel in line. When demand for oil is high they stick together; when demand is low the weaker members are tempted to give special offers in order to maintain their revenue. No cartel can be stronger than its weakest member.

In many parts of the world cartels are illegal. They nevertheless continue to exist in secret in many industries. (Trustbusters commonly find them in the chemicals, pharmaceuticals and financial industries.)

Part of the problem of identification is that the behaviour of a cartel can in many respects resemble the behaviour of a market under conditions of perfect competition. For example, when a number of banks change their interest rates identically, at the same time on the same day, who is to say that they do not do this because competition is fierce and they cannot afford to be out of line with each other for more than a morning? Yet they seem to be behaving just like a cartel.

CASCADING

A MARKETING STRATEGY in which a manufacturer penetrates a small market segment before cascading into other markets and market segments. It was a strategy often followed by large Japanese manufacturing firms. Honda, for instance, first went into the American market selling just small motorcycles. Gradually, however, it cascaded its whole range of products (including automobiles) into the market. The benefit of such a strategy is that it enables the manufacturer to set up an extensive distribution and servicing network without attracting too much attention.

Case-study method
Business schools have traditionally relied on the case-study method of teaching, and Harvard has been its greatest exponent. It involves detailed examination of business cases (that is, stories about corporate strategies, both real and imagined). The method has been criticised on several grounds.

- It is unreal. By and large, real business problems need to be solved "on the hoof" and in a hurry, not in a leisurely academic atmosphere.
- It can make business seem like little more than a series of problems looking for solutions.
- Cases are limited to those that the teaching staff have been able to put together. In many schools (including Harvard) this has made them to parochial. Students want more international material.

To help get round the last problem a number of clearing houses for case studies, such as the European Case Clearing House, have been set up. These enable BUSINESS SCHOOLS to purchase each other's material. To improve the quality there are a number of competitions, such as the annual European Case Writing Competition, giving prizes for the best-written case studies.

Cash cow
This is the type of business occupying the bottom left-hand corner of the BOSTON CONSULTING GROUP'S GROWTH SHARE MATRIX. It is a business with a high MARKET SHARE but low growth prospects. Companies are advised to use the cash produced by their cash cows to support their "stars" and their "question marks" (the businesses with high growth potential).

The idea seemed radical in its time because the temptation for managers is often to reinvest the surplus cash into the cash cow itself as a reward for its success. It feels intuitively wrong to "milk" a successful business in order to feed an as yet unsuccessful one.

The danger now, perhaps, is the other way round. Managers have become so familiar with the thinking behind the Boston matrix that they always starve the cash cow, ignoring any potential it may still have to be rejuvenated. There is an additional problem in persuading able career-oriented managers that a business already identified as a cash cow, good only for milking, is good enough for them to devote their full attention to.

CASHFLOW

The amount of cash coming into a business during a specified period of time – the cashflow equals the business's PROFIT with depreciation added back, although cashflow movements lag behind the profit figure on any particular day.

A strong cashflow has advantages and disadvantages. It releases a company from the exacting demands of the capital markets, but it raises the vexing question of what to do with the cash. Basically, there are four alternatives.

- To invest it in growing the core business.
- To invest it in other businesses. This has led to many a disastrous DIVERSIFICATION STRATEGY in the past. Too many companies have assumed that management is fungible, that it can be spread around any business willy-nilly.
- To keep it so that it earns interest. In this case the company is behaving like a bank, which is probably not what its shareholders would wish. Nevertheless, this option has proved popular because companies have in the past proved strangely reluctant to follow the fourth alternative.
- To distribute the surplus cash back to shareholders, either in the form of dividends or as more tax-efficient capital redistributions. If capital markets were truly

efficient this is what would happen. Shareholders would then be free to reinvest their money elsewhere, as and when they saw fit.

CASHFLOW STATEMENT

In many countries, companies must show in their annual accounts a statement of their CASHFLOW during the year, along with the PROFIT AND LOSS ACCOUNT (income statement) and the BALANCE SHEET. It is the third most significant corporate financial statement and one that has come in for an increasing amount of attention as people realise that a company's income statement can show a healthy profit for the year, although the company itself may not have the cash to survive. Previously known as the funds-flow statement or, in the UK, the statement of source and application of funds.

CAVEAT EMPTOR

Latin for "Let the buyer beware", a phrase that carried more weight before the spate of modern legislation designed to protect the consumer from the evil ways of wily businesses. In the old days, buyers purchased goods entirely at their own risk, without any express guarantee in the purchasing contract.

ALFRED CHANDLER

A pioneering management thinker whose classic book, *Strategy and Structure*, was first published in 1966. Chandler was an early proponent of DECENTRALISATION, arguing that STRATEGY was the responsibility of head office, but the day-to-day running of an organisation's operations should be left to decentralised and comparatively autonomous business units.

CHANGE MANAGEMENT

The GLOBALISATION of business and rapid leaps in technology (especially in INFORMATION TECHNOLOGY) brought home to managers at the end of the 20th century that they had to change their view of change itself. Traditionally, managers viewed corporations as static entities (or at least as entities in search of a static state), but they were increasingly pressed to see them as dynamic organisations in a constant state of flux. This meant discarding much management thinking, including many ideas about long-term planning, for example.

Learning to live with change is for some people almost counter-intuitive. Managers have always been conservative by nature and, by definition, have abhorred change. Their abhorrence was largely born out of fear: the fear of failure, and the fear of going beyond a point of no return.

Awareness of the permanence of change is no longer new, however. What may be new is an awareness that change is not even a process of evolution towards permanence. Companies are simply wasting their time if they are looking for a fixed state in which all need for further change has been removed.

Surrounded by the increasingly shabby remnants of a dwindling inheritance, they could not bring themselves at a moment of crisis to surrender their memories and alter the unique pattern of their lives.

J.H. Elliott, *Imperial Spain*

CHERRY-PICKING

The idea of buying (or selling) separately a number of products or services that have traditionally been bought (or sold) together. In the insurance market, for instance, the firm that offers car insurance only to women is cherry-picking, because women drivers make fewer and smaller claims than men. Cherry-picking disrupts the whole market and can revolutionise the MARKET SHARE of the different players within it.

CHINESE WALLS

The internal barriers that companies put up between different departments to ensure that no information passes illegally from one to another. The expression applies particularly to financial institutions, such as banks, where the MERGERS AND

ACQUISITIONS department might be working on a TAKEOVER deal which, if it were known to the fund-management department, could result in them making a considerable gain from the illegal use of inside information.

Code of conduct
A set of rules drawn up to guide the behaviour of a profession or industry. The rules are usually devised by industry associations (in such businesses as travel or insurance) to protect their general interest against the individual rogue who can threaten to throw them all into disrepute. Codes of conduct may also be imposed by industry regulators (such as central banks in the case of commercial banking) or by governments (for monopolies such as telecoms).

Company MBA
A tailor-made MBA run by an individual company for the benefit of its own employees and designed to meet the complaint that too many of the business schools' off-the-peg courses are too theoretical. To receive academic recognition, however, such MBAS have to be run in conjunction with a qualified BUSINESS SCHOOL.

The advantage of company MBAS is that they can be designed to meet the needs of a particular business. In the UK, for example, W.H. Smith, a bookseller and stationer, ran a company MBA that concentrated on the skills needed to MANAGE one of its own high-street shops. This isn't much use, of course, if the employee subsequently wants to go and work for a biotech company.

Comparative advantage
An economic idea first propounded by an economist, David Ricardo, in the early 19th century, a time when arguments in favour of free trade were not taken so much for granted as they are today.

The principle of comparative advantage says that the world will be better off if each country concentrates on producing what it does best, even if what it does second-best is better than what another country does best. Production will be maximised if each country concentrates on what it is best fitted to produce, and then all trade their goods among themselves.

Competitive advantage
The idea that companies' strengths and weaknesses can only be measured relative to those of their competitors. For example, what good is a 20% increase in PRODUCTIVITY at Philips if Sony has a 30% increase over the same period?

The theory of competitive advantage is particularly associated with a Harvard academic, MICHAEL PORTER. It says, in effect, that there are no absolutes. A company is good at manufacturing when (and only when) it has a competitive advantage over other manufacturers. Such an advantage can lie in many things: lower costs because of greater computerisation and lower wage bills; more reliable machinery; better QUALITY CONTROL; cheaper borrowing; and so on. This has led companies to pay more attention to comparing their performance with that of their rivals rather than with that old favourite, their own performance in a previous period.

Concentration
The degree to which an industry is controlled by a few firms. This is usually measured by the percentage of the industry's total turnover that is in the hands of the four largest firms in the business (known as the C4 ratio), the five largest (known as the C5), or the eight largest (C8). Another measure is the HERFINDAHL INDEX.

It is important for companies to monitor concentration ratios in their own industry to discover whether their market is turning into an OLIGOPOLY, in which case they will have to adjust their STRATEGY. It is also important for them to know whether their customers' (or their suppliers') industries are becoming more concentrated, for that will give them more or less power in their buying or selling.

CONCESSION

A special right given to somebody, usually for a price, not always paid in cash. For example:

- the exclusive right to sell the products of a manufacturer within a certain geographical area;
- the right to dig for minerals on a particular plot of land;
- a tax allowance to encourage things like exports and investment in underdeveloped regions.

CONGLOMERATE

A company that is in a large number of different businesses, not all of which seem to fit logically with each other. Such companies present a challenge to journalists' descriptive powers. "The fags-to-bags group" is one attempt for B.A.T, which makes cigarettes and paper (and lots of other things as well).

CONSORTIUM

The combination of a number of large companies for the purposes of one specific project. This occurs commonly with large building projects, such as dams and bridges, which are too big for one company to undertake alone. Consortia are useful too when the range of specialist skills that are needed for a job cannot be found within a single company.

CONSORTIUM MBA

These MBA courses take students solely from a small group of organisations that have sponsored the course at a particular academic institution. The course is then a part-time or block MBA in which students retain close links with their sponsor, who is probably also their employer. A student's project work on a consortium MBA will normally be undertaken for the sponsor. Sponsors (and there may be as many as 20 of them) have considerable influence on the content and structure of the course and aim to make sure that it is relevant to their needs. For the students, this almost inevitably means that the course will not be as broad in scope as a conventional MBA.

CONSUMER CHOICE
Consumers have choices, and increasingly so. What influences these choices is the subject of MARKETING. It can be price or quality, or it can be a BRAND. Whatever it is that persuades a consumer to choose to buy one firm's product rather than another's is a thing of great VALUE.

CONTINGENT LIABILITY
A liability that may arise if something else happens. One example would be a company that currently had a lawsuit against it claiming that it had polluted a large area of land. If found liable, the company could face a huge bill for the cost of repairing the damage. In its annual report to shareholders the company might want to mention that it has such a liability, contingent upon the outcome of the lawsuit.

CONTINUOUS IMPROVEMENT
The English translation of the Japanese term *kaizen*. The drive for continuous improvement, originally applied to manufacturing quality, has broadened in scope to include all business PROCESSES. The focus is on making small but cumulative improvements that add up over time to a substantial COMPETITIVE ADVANTAGE.

CONTROL SYSTEM
A method of ensuring that certain production and management processes are carried out properly and on time. They may be mechanical systems built into production lines to measure and control the flow of semi-finished goods from one PROCESS to another, or they may be computer programs built into information systems to remind managers, for example, of sales targets that they are scheduled to reach.

Convergence

The coming together of different industries so that, for example, banking is available in supermarkets and the INTERNET can be viewed on television. Convergence has been brought about largely by the rapid development of INFORMATION TECHNOLOGY. Supermarkets' card-based electronic payment systems are the beginnings of a bank. The telephone-based Internet can provide screen images that begin to look like TV programmes.

Core competence

The skill that is at the heart of a company's business, and that over-diversified companies are being encouraged to return to. A core competence need not necessarily be narrow. Honda, a Japanese company, sees its core competence to be the manufacture of fuel-powered engines; from there it has built an industry that manufactures cars, motorbikes and lawnmowers. Procter & Gamble might argue that its core competence does not lie in its manufacturing processes at all, but in its ability to market FAST-MOVING CONSUMER GOODS, in which case it makes sense for it to move from making washing powder to making toothpaste.

Gary Hamel and C.K. Prahalad, writing in the *Harvard Business Review*, have described three essential elements of a core competence.

- It should provide potential access to a wide variety of markets.
- It should make a significant contribution to the perceived customer benefits of the end products.
- It should be difficult for competitors to imitate.

Corporate culture

The distinctive behaviour patterns that give a corporation its individual identity. These can be powerful motivators (or otherwise) of the workforce, and they are greatly influenced by the local culture in which a company mainly operates. For example, the computer companies of California's

Silicon Valley set a new laid-back corporate culture for all industry in that region.

Corporate culture has become of greater significance with GLOBALISATION. Companies have found that they cannot transplant their culture willy-nilly across the globe. They have had to be like chameleons and adapt to the local culture of the many places in which they have set up.

Some still deny that culture has any significance for a corporation. One American manager claimed that the only culture in his organisation was in the yoghurts in the canteen. However, most managers now believe that culture (that is, an organisation's distinctive pattern of ideas and behaviour) does matter. In their book *In Search of Excellence*, TOM PETERS and Robert Waterman found that "the dominance and coherence of culture proved to be an essential quality of excellent companies".

Culture is the collective programming of the mind which distinguishes the members of one human group from another.

Geert Hofstede

Corporate finance

That part of investment or merchant banking that is directed at helping companies to identify what their financial needs are, and then arranging to satisfy them.

Corporate governance

The manner in which corporations are governed; something that differs greatly from country to country. In Anglo-Saxon economies, the ultimate authority is given to shareholders, the owners of the corporation, who take risks with their money.

Anglo-Saxon corporate empire builders have grown by setting out to satisfy shareholders first and last. In such societies, hostile TAKEOVERS occur as struggles between competing sets of shareholders. Other constituencies of STAKEHOLDERS in the corporation – employees, suppliers, creditors and customers – can but watch and wait.

In Germany and Japan, corporate governance is rather different. Other constituencies (particularly employees and banks) have a greater say in the corporation's future (through works' councils, or representation on the BOARD, or through Japan's unique process of consensus forming). In these countries, hostile takeovers are frowned upon and (though decreasingly so) still often resisted.

The man who is denied the opportunity of taking decisions of importance begins to regard as important the decisions that he is allowed to take.
C. Northcote Parkinson

CORPORATE PLANNING
A system to help managers decide how to allocate scarce resources among different parts of their organisation, designed specifically for the large diversified corporations built up in the 1960s and 1970s. The process of corporate planning encouraged the growth of centralisation within these diversified corporations. But with the break-up of many CONGLOMERATES in more recent years, and the popularity of DECENTRALISATION, the role of corporate planning has become much diminished.

COST-BENEFIT ANALYSIS
The calculation of the benefit to customers accruing from a particular cost; for example, how much extra will consumers pay to get a guaranteed same-day postal delivery service from within the same city? Is the benefit to be gained from the premium price that can be charged for the service higher than the cost of setting up the service?

Cost-benefit analysis is not a difficult concept to grasp. The problem arises in practice, in deciding which costs to include in the analysis (should there be a contribution from the overhead costs of all the postal services in the above example?), and which benefits to include (how do you measure the favourable feeling of customers towards the postal service for providing a new service designed just for them?).

COST CENTRE
A unit to which the specific costs of a business can be allocated. This can be something as small as an individual machine. The importance of allocating costs correctly to different centres is an important prerequisite in the formation of any STRATEGY. If a company does not know where its costs arise, it does not know where its PROFITS arise.

COST OF CAPITAL
Superficially, a fairly easy calculation of the relative costs of different types of capital, such as loans, equity, bonds, and so on. The cost of equity is the dividend, and the cost of the rest is interest. The first complication comes from taxation, which can put the net cost of equity on a par with the gross cost of loans. Then there is the question of the degree of flexibility that corporations have in altering dividend payments. Cutting the dividend does not necessarily reduce the cost of capital. If the company is quoted, then the stockmarket is sure to mark down the price of the company's shares as a consequence, and that presents an extra cost.

COST STRUCTURE
The allocation of a company's costs between fixed, variable and MARGINAL COSTS. A company with high fixed costs will have a higher BARRIER TO EXIT than will a company with lower fixed costs. This has implications for the company itself, and for all its competitors. It means, for example, that a company should beware of entering a market where all the participants have high fixed costs.

CPA
See CRITICAL PATH ANALYSIS.

CREDIT CONTROL
The process of controlling the amount of credit that a company grants to its customers in order to improve its CASHFLOW and to reduce the value of its bad debts. A reduction of one day in the average outstanding period of a company's creditors can

make the difference between a sound business and a wobbly one.

CRISIS MANAGEMENT

Any company is vulnerable to a sudden disaster that can threaten its whole business. For example, the poisonous gases that escaped from Union Carbide's plant at Bhopal in India killing thousands of people in 1984; or the small quantities of carcinogenic benzene that were found in Perrier's water source in the 1990s. Both were events that overnight threatened huge companies with disaster. How should companies MANAGE such a crisis?

Most large companies now have a contingency plan for dealing with disasters. Here are the widely copied guidelines devised by one company (a subsidiary of Warner-Lambert).

- Speed is of the essence, and the first few days' behaviour is vital.
- Do not overreact.
- Stay close to your market.
- Watch the competition's reaction.
- Be prepared to yield some of your market initially.
- Do not assume a hostile environment.
- Build GOODWILL before the crisis; it will stand you in good stead later.

CRITICAL PATH ANALYSIS

An analysis of the slowest elements that have to occur in sequence in any particular series of business PROCESSES or activities. The addition of the time taken to perform each of the elements in the sequence is the minimum time that it will take to implement the whole operation. For example, when building a house there are certain things that cannot happen until others have happened: plastering has to take place after the wiring; walls cannot be built until the foundations are in place. Other things, such as roofing and wiring, can go on simultaneously.

Critical path analysis (CPA) is often more important as a method of realising which actions depend on others than as a way of finding out how long it will take to complete a complex task.

Critical success factors

Those elements in a business that are most critical to its success. In a DOT COM business, for example, it may be the links that the business can make with other WEBSITES; in a pizza delivery service it might be the speed of delivery (and not, surprisingly, the quality of the pizza). Identifying the business's critical success factors (CSFS) enables it to understand (and then to ignore) those factors that are not critical to its success.

CRM

See CUSTOMER RELATIONSHIP MANAGEMENT.

Cross-subsidisation

The practice of selling one product at a loss in order to sell more of another at a profit. Consider razors and razor blades. Suppose (as has long been the case) that the PROFIT margins on razors are thin, but those on blades are fat. If a company can sell a lot of razors of a type that can use only its make of blade, then it would be an excellent idea to market the razors aggressively, even by selling them at below cost, in order to sell (later) a lot of profitable blades. Similarly, in the computer industry, as long as one manufacturer's products were not compatible with those of any other manufacturer, it made sense for companies to sell the initial hardware at cost price (or below) in order to tie customers in to buying further products in their range.

The danger with cross-subsidisation is that it is a system of "give now, take later". A company can find that its industry has evolved in such a way that when it is time to take, the opportunity has disappeared. With computers, for example, any one manufacturer's models are increasingly compatible with any other's. Suppose in such a situation that a manufacturer has sold its basic PC at cost, and that by the time the customer is ready to buy add-ons, other manufacturers are producing them at much lower margins. The original manufacturer may then find that there is no profit in any part of its computer operation.

CSF

See CRITICAL SUCCESS FACTORS.

CUSTOMER RELATIONSHIP MANAGEMENT

The management of a firm's relationships with its customers has become a central concern of business in the 21st century. Customer relationship management (CRM) is the shorthand for this belated recognition of the importance of customers to business success. It is, says one consultant, a matter of "identifying, attracting and retaining the most valuable customers to sustain profitable growth". The development of sophisticated computer databases has enabled large companies to handle their customer relations with all the intimacy of a corner shop. They can identify and acknowledge birthdays and other significant dates, and they can propose special offers that meet needs identified by the database.

CUSTOMISATION

The processes that turn traditionally mass-produced goods into products styled to meet the needs of individual customers. Thus Levi's customised its mass-produced jeans by taking an individual customer's measurements in a shop and passing them (by computer) on to a central manufacturing unit where they were read by machines that then cut and sewed the garment. Before MASS-PRODUCTION processes were introduced, most goods were customised.

Data mining

The analysis of large volumes of data in order to find relationships between different variables. In particular, data mining is increasingly being used in MARKETING to identify customers that might be of value, often by uncovering previously unknown relationships. For example, if you are opening a flower shop in town X you might want to "mine" into a database to find the names and addresses of all the people who live within a ten-mile radius of X and have a birthday within the next three weeks. You might in the process discover that people who buy petrol on Friday evenings also often buy flowers.

Data protection

With an increasing amount of information about individuals held on computer databases, most countries have introduced so-called data-protection legislation to give individuals the right to have access (on request) to data that is held about them on central computers. Data protection is increasingly relevant to the INTERNET, where an individual's personal details can be zapped around the world at the click of a mouse.

Data warehousing

The orderly organisation of electronic data within a corporation's IT systems so that it can be used effectively by different parts of the corporation. In this way, employees in charge of new products, say, can have direct, real-time access to information about the sales of existing products. It may sound somewhat surprising that it was not ever thus.

DCF

See DISCOUNTED CASHFLOW.

Edward de Bono

An unconventional guru, born in Malta, who is best known as the inventor of the concept of LATERAL THINKING. This is now defined as "seeking to solve problems by unorthodox or apparently illogical means".

In the management field, De Bono's work has been focused on trying to persuade managers to think "outside the box" (beyond the norm). Most managers, he believes, are trained to maintain things efficiently and to solve problems. Seeking new business opportunities requires a different set of thinking skills.

An opportunity is not there until after you have seen it.
Edward de Bono

DECENTRALISATION
The process of distributing power away from the centre of large organisations and out to semi-autonomous divisions. The idea was popularised by the two Alfreds.

- ALFRED CHANDLER, a business historian whose book *Strategy and Structure* looked at decentralisation as a corporate structure particularly suited to the geographically and commercially diversified CONGLOMERATES that grew up after the second world war.
- Alfred Sloan, the chairman for many years of General Motors, whose book *My Years with General Motors* described putting into effect what he called "federal decentralisation" at the then fast-growing car company in the 1920s.

Chandler's book came out in 1962 and Sloan's in 1963. For the rest of that decade companies busily considered how best to decentralise. For the most part, however, they took decentralisation only so far. Operational responsibilities were devolved to divisional managers in the field, but strategic management was maintained firmly at the centre: a combination of centralisation and decentralisation within the same organisation.

DECISION TREE
A graphic representation of the various options

flowing from an initial decision. A decision tree might, for example, be drawn up by a merchant banker reviewing the possible courses of action following a TAKEOVER bid. A number of branches will spread out from each decision point, creating the appearance of a tree.

Declining industry

An industry whose market seems to be contracting inevitably and irreversibly; for example, the markets for vinyl records and audio tapes. Declining industries present managers with a formidable question: what should they do about their existing CAPACITY in the market? A classic MARKETING response is to harvest the product for all it is worth by raising prices, cutting ADVERTISING expenditure, pruning product lines, and so on. Another option is to invest in PROMOTION with an eye to obtaining leadership of whatever is left of the market when (and if) it stops declining.

The STRATEGY to be followed depends largely on the company's view of the decline. Few declines are inevitable, and even fewer are predictable before they happen. None are smooth while they are happening. Action has to be determined partly by what rivals in the market are doing at the same time. If they are cutting capacity rapidly in a bolt for the exit, then it may be prudent to aim for leadership of a shrunken market. Alternatively, if the BARRIERS TO EXIT are high, it may be better just to harvest what is left as fast as possible.

Delayering

Removing layers of management from the middle levels of a corporation (see FLAT ORGANISATION).

W. Edwards Deming

An American consultant who taught quality management to the Japanese soon after the end of the second world war, at a time when (believe it or not) "Made in Japan" meant junk. Deming taught the Japanese that "the consumer is the most important part of the production line", and he taught them to use statistical methods to control the quality of their production. They learned his lessons well.

In 1951 the Japanese established the Deming Prize, a now prestigious annual award given to the company that has done the most in applying statistical methods to its QUALITY CONTROL. For many years Deming was unappreciated in his home country, but in his old age he became much in demand in the United States as well.

If I had to reduce my message for management to just a few words, I'd say it all had to do with reducing variation.

W. Edwards Deming

DEMOGRAPHICS

The distribution of human populations according to age, sex, race, and so on. An important part of the MARKETING of any product or service is an understanding of the demographics of the market in which it is to be sold. It is no good trying to sell yoghurt to ethnic groups whose adults cannot digest milk products.

Clever marketing often depends on spotting demographic changes at an early stage. Two recent demographic changes have provided some exciting marketing opportunities.

- A sharp fall in the birth rate in many developed countries. This has led some north European countries to experience a decline in their total population; that is, there are fewer births than deaths, a situation unknown in Europe since before the second world war. Combined with an increase in longevity, this has turned marketers' attention away from the cult of youth to the cult of age. Growth industries have been in leisure and in health care.
- A shrinking in the average size of the family unit. This has come about because of the high divorce rate, later marriage and the greater mobility of individuals. It has

provided opportunities in the food industry for things like ready meals for singles.

Deregulation
Literally, the removal of regulations. In the 1980s deregulation became a sort of faith that cemented the supply-side economists of the Reagan and Thatcher years. Among the first industries to be deregulated under their influence were the American airlines. Rules governing the routes that airlines could fly and the prices that they could charge were lifted. For a while there was a flurry of activity. Ten years later, however, the industry resembled nothing so much as its pre-deregulation self. A not dissimilar analysis can be applied to some other industries that have been enthusiastically deregulated – banking, for instance.

Differentiation
The process of identifying the way in which a company's products differ from its rivals' products, and then establishing that difference in the consumer's mind by suitable ADVERTISING and PROMOTION. Underlying this is an appreciation that it is easier to sell something that is differentiable from other products on the market than it is to sell something that duplicates an existing product. Differentiation provides an added service to the customer for which the manufacturer can charge a premium. New tastes (like the fashion for health foods and concern for the environment) provide all sorts of opportunities for differentiation.

Diminishing returns
The economic principle that as more resources are put into a project the less are the resulting increases in output. When workers start a job they are reasonably productive; as they warm up they reach their peak PRODUCTIVITY; then, as they get tired, the law of diminishing returns sets in. For every hour's work they do thereafter they produce less. Diminishing returns are almost the opposite of ECONOMIES OF SCALE and, indeed, are sometimes known as diseconomies of scale.

DIRECT MAIL
A method of selling goods and services by sending catalogues, leaflets and other pieces of paper through the post. Sometimes known as junk mail, there is a widespread (but false) belief that only paper companies benefit from direct mail. In practice, it provides manufacturers with a way of targeting their audience more precisely than they can by using traditional ADVERTISING channels.

DIRECT MARKETING
The selling of goods and services in the most direct way possible. Thus the farmer who sells his produce on a market stall at the weekends directly to customers is engaging in direct marketing. Any form of selling that cuts out intermediaries (like retailers) can be described as direct marketing – telephone selling, for instance, and mail order.

DIRECTOR
A person appointed by shareholders to look after their interests in the management of their company. The directors as a body constitute the BOARD of a company. Company directors are restricted in what they can do. In general, they cannot make contracts with the company and they cannot take loans from the company (unless the company is itself in the business of making loans). If a company is deemed to have been trading when it was technically insolvent, the directors can become personally liable for its debts. One of the few benefits for directors is that they are free effectively to fix their own remuneration.

The term director is also used more loosely in the titles of senior management posts; for example, MARKETING director, human resources director. Such directors may well not have a seat on a board. (See also NON-EXECUTIVE DIRECTOR.)

DISCLOSURE
The disclosure of information by companies is a source of constant tension. Various authorities (government departments, and so on) demand it, and so do the general public (as consumers, and

also increasingly as partakers of the same environment). Yet most companies would (given the choice) prefer not to reveal it; not because they are up to no good, but because of the COMPETITIVE ADVANTAGE that information gives to their rivals. At least for as long as their rivals are publishing as much information as they are, the game is being played on a level playing field.

In most countries, certain disclosure requirements are obligatory.

- All companies have to file annual accounts; in the majority of cases a PROFIT AND LOSS ACCOUNT and a BALANCE SHEET, and, increasingly, a CASHFLOW STATEMENT.
- Quoted companies have to file further information with stock-exchange authorities when they want to raise money on the capital markets. In the United States, the authority is the Securities and Exchange Commission (SEC). For many companies, foreign ones in particular, the disclosure requirements of the SEC are a serious deterrent to obtaining a quotation in New York. The cost of producing the information required can be truly prohibitive.

DISCOUNTED CASHFLOW

A method of calculating the present VALUE of a future stream of income and capital (the CASHFLOW). Discounted cashflow is used to compare different expected RATES OF RETURN on different projects. It is based on discounting back future flows of cash in order to determine their NET PRESENT VALUE. This makes them of the same genus, so they can be added to and subtracted from each other. It provides a framework for answering questions such as: suppose an investment of $100 in project A is expected to bring in $10 at the end of year one and $110 at the end of year two. Alternatively, investing $100 in project B is expected to bring in nothing at the end of year one but $125 at the end of year two. Which project gives the better rate of return?

DISINTERMEDIATION
The process whereby financial intermediaries (like banks) get chopped out of the chain that passes money from an original lender to an ultimate borrower. Disintermediation is encouraged by the large margins that banks maintain on their lending. It has accelerated in recent years for the following reasons.

- The creation and growth of new financial instruments like commercial paper have encouraged companies to invest their short-term cash in tradable instruments rather than leaving it in bank deposits.
- Companies have begun to lend directly among themselves: from company B, which has surplus cash, to company A, which does not.

DISTANCE LEARNING
The lonely business of learning at a long distance from the institution that is teaching you. Distance learning is being promoted as the best way to overcome the imbalance between the demand for MBAS and the supply of good courses and teachers. It has been helped by new technologies; in particular, the INTERNET and the videocassette recorder.

Not all distance learning is passive. The teaching material can include interactive software programs that require students to respond, and then give them feedback. A major benefit of distance-learning programmes is that students can progress at their own pace, uninterrupted by shuffling and snuffling in the row behind.

DISTRIBUTION
The process of getting products from factory to consumer. This often involves a complicated distribution system consisting of wholesalers, retailers and other middlemen. These people sort, store, ship and finance the products on their way to the final consumer.

Distribution can also refer to a measure of MARKET PENETRATION – the number of retail outlets that stock a particular product expressed as a percentage of all the outlets that could possibly sell that product.

DISTRIBUTION CHANNEL

The routes, both physical and managerial, by which a product travels from manufacturer to consumer. So integrated is the world's economy today that any product can be distributed anywhere at almost any time. Fresh flowers in Paris on a winter's day were growing in Madagascar at the beginning of the week; apples in New York in December were on a branch in Chile in November.

INFORMATION TECHNOLOGY has shifted the direction of many distribution channels in recent years. For example, use of the INTERNET to order groceries threatens to remove the supremacy of the out-of-town supermarket and its huge car parks, and replace them with central warehouses and fleets of small vans delivering direct to the customer's door.

DIVERSIFICATION

A corporate STRATEGY that was popular in the 1960s and 1970s. Diversification was based on the belief that it was not wise to have too much business in one business, that every corporation should have a diversified portfolio of businesses. Between 1960 and 1980 the percentage of American companies in the *Fortune 500* that were diversified increased from 50% to 80%. The specific reasons given for diversification were varied.

- To be in counter-cyclical businesses that would carry the corporation through bad years.
- To use a core of management skills that could be turned to almost anything; that is, if a company were good at finding and selling oil it would be good at finding and selling copper.
- To balance businesses that generated a lot of cash with businesses that needed a lot of cash, so that the company could act as a sort of surrogate bank.

In the 1980s diversification went out of fashion, and diversified companies sold off much of their portfolio of businesses. For example, a British company, Reed, started the 1960s as a paper manufacturer. It diversified from there into packaging, printing and publishing. (One chief executive said that the only thing these businesses had in common was the fact that they all began with the letter P.) Then it sold off all its businesses except publishing.

Dot com

The spoken version of the .com INTERNET address. Originally, the address was used to denote a commercial site (as opposed to .org, which was the suffix for non-profit organisations). However, dot com came to be used to refer to those Internet-based businesses that briefly, at the turn of the century, were able to command huge prices on the stockmarket on the basis of little more than a wing and a prayer. Few if any of them needed to prove they could make profits before investors were prepared to throw millions their way.

Double-entry book-keeping

The fundamental principle of book-keeping, and therefore of accounting, that every entry in a company's books has an equal and opposite counterpart. Every transaction that a company effects creates an ASSET on one side of the ledger, and an equal and opposite LIABILITY on the other. This duality of business transactions means that a company's books must always balance; that is, the monetary VALUE of each side of the ledger must be equal. This is the origin of the expression BALANCE SHEET. The origin of double-entry book-keeping is usually attributed to 14th-century Italy.

Double-loop learning

A concept closely associated with the writing of CHRIS ARGYRIS. Single-loop learning is what happens when employees correct errors without changing the corporate norms that allowed the errors to happen in the first place. Double-loop learning occurs when errors are corrected by examining and altering the norms first, and then the erroneous action. Only in this way does the company retain the lesson that the employee learned, even after the employee has gone to work elsewhere.

Downmarket

A MARKETING term that assumes that markets have a top and a bottom, and that products continually move upmarket towards the top, or downmarket towards the bottom. It is not always clear what scale this top and bottom are part of. Is it the price of the product, the social class of the buyer, or the exclusivity of the product? Is a basic Rolls-Royce a downmarket product? Is every shop in Gstaad upmarket?

Downsize

An expression used to refer to a wholesale reduction in the size of a company's workforce, something that occurred in many large companies in the early 1990s. Downsizing has often consisted of a combination of redundancy and OUTSOURCING, where functions traditionally carried on inside the company have been handed over to an outside specialist. Downsizing fell out of favour as companies that downsized found themselves losing employees with skills that were difficult to replace. The result was a shift in emphasis to rightsizing, that is, taking steps to make sure the organisation has the appropriate number of employees with the appropriate skills.

Downstream

All manufacturing of goods and all provision of services can be seen as a series of links in a chain, from the digging up of raw materials to the adding of bar codes at the final retail outlet. In an analogy with rivers, those links that are near the source of the operation (such as the digging of raw materials) are said to be upstream; those links that are near the mouth of the river (that is, close to the ocean of consumers) are said to be downstream.

Companies can then be defined as having a centre of gravity that is either upstream or downstream. Oil companies are a classic example of upstream businesses that have attempted to move downstream, first by refining oil into other oil products and then by moving into the manufacture of petrochemicals. Most companies seeking to diversify first look immediately upstream, or immediately downstream, of their centres of gravity.

Downtime

Originally, the amount of paid time that employees spent not working because they lacked the necessary materials, or because their machinery was being serviced. In old-established American and European plants, this could be as much as 20% of the working week.

Japanese methods of production have reduced the amounts of downtime to an absolute minimum, and the word has taken on a new meaning in the world of computers. There it refers to the amount of time lost because a computer is not working expressed as a percentage of the total amount of time it was planned that it should work.

Peter Drucker

Described by the magazine *Business Week* as "the most read, most listened to, most regarded guru in management", Peter Drucker has had a profound effect on businesses all over the world. Born in Austria, his early careers were in journalism and banking before he emigrated to the United States in 1937. There he stayed to one side of the BUSINESS SCHOOL mainstream, preferring to express his thinking outside the straitjacket of management academics. Like many original thinkers, his ideas (on the customer-driven business, for example) soon came to seem as if they had always been there.

His description of the seven tasks of the manager of the future (taken from his book *The Practice of Management*, published in 1954) have become a classic touchstone. Managers, he said, must:

- MANAGE by objectives;
- take more risks, and risks will have to be taken at lower levels of the organisation;
- make strategic decisions;
- be able to build integrated teams;
- be able to communicate information quickly and clearly;
- be able to see how their job fits into the business as a whole;
- be able to see how the business fits into the general political, economic and social environment, both at home and abroad.

DUE DILIGENCE
The process of checking to see that a company's books are as the company claims they are before the company is taken over. The job, carried out by accountants, is a delicate one. Companies are reluctant to reveal their all to suitors in case the suitors do not like what they see, and then go away with nothing but the inside knowledge of a business that they did not buy.

DUMPING
The process of selling goods in a foreign market at prices that are below cost, or below the price for which they are being sold in their domestic market. Such activity is unpopular in most places and illegal in some. It is usually assumed to be something that East Asian manufacturers do to European and North American markets. However, the South Koreans have accused the French of dumping cement in their market, and the South Koreans have in turn been accused by the Japanese of dumping textiles.

EARNINGS PER SHARE
A popular yardstick of a company's performance over time – its total earnings (its net profit during a period) divided by the number of ordinary shares in issue. Earnings per share (EPS) also provides a way of comparing one company's performance with another's.

E-COMMERCE
Electronic commerce, essentially the buying and selling of goods and services via the INTERNET. Pioneers of e-commerce, such as the bookseller Amazon, have been successful in building revenue from e-commerce, but not so far in converting the dramatic potential of this new medium into profits. (See also B2B and B2C.)

ECONOMIC VALUE ADDED
The after-tax CASHFLOW that a company earns from its invested capital, minus the cost of that capital. Economic value added (EVA) is a popular yardstick for measuring the VALUE added by an investment or business decision.

ECONOMIES OF SCALE
One of the most fundamental ideas in the economics of the firm, and one of the most misunderstood: the larger the quantity of a product or service that is produced, the lower is the AVERAGE COST per unit. This occurs because fixed costs can be spread more widely. Thus a given amount of ADVERTISING can be spread more thinly (in terms of cost per unit) over a product of which 10X are sold than over a product of which only X are sold. Economies of scale also arise from the fact that some (efficient) technologies can be applied only above a certain production level – for example, large transport systems or continuous production lines.

If economies of scale could be applied *ad infinitum*, then all firms would aim to grow indefinitely. But they have their limits. Above a certain size diseconomies of scale begin to set in. The sheer cost of managing so many people and so much equipment begins to offset the advantages of adding yet another production line, and so on. These diseconomies are sometimes called the costs of complexity.

Economies of scope
This is a slightly different concept from ECONOMIES OF SCALE. It is the savings in unit cost that come from producing or supplying a range of products (as opposed to a larger quantity of the same product). The savings in this case come in distribution, R&D and central services such as accounting and public relations. Economies of scope often underlie the reasons given for DIVERSIFICATION. Japanese electronics companies like Hitachi and Matsushita manufacture photocopiers, fax machines, telephones, printers and personal computers, because all these products are aimed at the same market of office equipment users.

Earnout
A way of bridging the difference between what vendors believe will be their companies' future profits and what purchasers expect them to be. An earnout is a way of paying for a company based on its future performance. The purchase price is a combination of an immediate up-front payment and a number of future payments related to future performance.

Elasticity
A measure of the relationship between two economic variables. How much one changes given a certain change in the other; for example, the price elasticity of demand. If a 1% change in the price of an item results in more than a 1% change in demand then the relationship is elastic. If the price change is less than 1% the relationship is said to be inelastic.

E-mail
Electronic mail, the communication of messages via the INTERNET. The use of e-mail has grown dramatically in recent years. Company managers now

communicate among themselves by e-mail as much as they used to by fax and by phone. But sending e-mail is not like sending letters or faxes: e-mail messages are read in a different way and interpreted in a different way. Messages on a screen are not valued by the recipient as highly as those on paper.

EMBA

See EXECUTIVE MBA.

EMPOWERMENT

The granting to all the employees within an organisation of the power to act on their own initiative as far as possible. Empowerment is an idea associated particularly with the work of Rosabeth Moss Kanter, a sociologist and management teacher who argues that only those companies that can empower all the individuals within their organisation stand a chance of winning in the "corporate Olympics". Too many employees, she argues, still need the "crutch" of hierarchy to empower them.

> *The powerless live in a different world … they may turn to the ultimate weapon of those who lack productive power: oppressive power.*
>
> Rosabeth Moss Kanter

END-USER

The final consumer who actually uses a product or service. This may not be the same person who is responsible for making the decision to purchase the product. The purchaser is the customer; the end-user is the consumer. This is an important distinction in MARKETING. Babies are the end-users of baby foods. They are not, however, the people who decide which baby foods to buy.

ENTREPRENEUR

A term that started off with a specific economic meaning: an individual who organises the FACTORS OF PRODUCTION (land, labour and capital), the risk-taker in business. Some economists consider the entrepreneur to be a fourth factor of production, without which the other three cannot produce anything. These economists, however, cannot have experienced Europe's nationalised industries, many of which carry on producing things without there being an entrepreneur in sight.

The term has come to have a wider meaning, referring to anybody with the qualities of leadership and adaptability that are considered essential to the creation of wealth. Much effort has gone into trying to identify these people, to nurture and encourage them with tax breaks, and to support them within large organisations.

I think if we want to understand the entrepreneur, we should look at the juvenile delinquent.

Abraham Zaleznik

Environmental audit

A method of ensuring that systems which minimise a company's adverse impact on the environment are in place and working, and that the company is continually complying with environmental legislation. Environmental audits were first introduced in the early 1970s, mostly by companies in the chemicals and petrochemicals industries. Large companies in environmentally sensitive businesses (such as BP and Royal Dutch/Shell) regularly carry out environmental audits. At Shell, teams of 3–5 people examine sites about once a year. Their work is confidential and internal (non-Shell employees are not involved). Many companies, however, bring in outside consultants for their environmental audits. BP widens its audit to look at a different issue each year.

EPS

See EARNINGS PER SHARE.

Euromarket

A market for financial instruments that are denominated in currencies held outside their country of issue. Thus a dollar-denominated corporate bond issued by a German company would be a Eurobond, a bond issued on the Euromarket. It should not be confused with a euro bond, a bond issued in the multinational currency unit of Western Europe.

EVA

See ECONOMIC VALUE ADDED.

EXCELLENCE

A school of management thinking clustered around (and inspired by) *In Search of Excellence*, a best-selling book written by TOM PETERS and Robert Waterman and published in 1982. The book marked a shift from thinking about management as a largely quantitative exercise in planning and efficiency to thinking about it as a qualitative process aimed first and foremost at satisfying customers. It changed management from being an introverted subject concerned with the internal workings of the organisation to an extrovert one that looked at the organisation in its wider context.

There are no excellent companies.
Tom Peters, *Thriving on Chaos*

EXCHANGE RISK

The risk that a business takes when it buys or sells goods or services at prices denominated in a currency other than its own. For exporters this is normal practice, and there are ways for them to reduce the risk (by HEDGING it).

Exporters who expect to receive a payment in a foreign currency at a future date can sell the currency forward at an agreed rate in exchange for their own currency. This reduces the intervening uncertainty. Many companies, from the very biggest to the very smallest, have come unstuck because they have preferred to take an exchange risk (in the hope of making a big gain from intervening shifts in exchange rates) rather than to cover their foreign exchange exposure. One of the big benefits of a single EU currency is the consequent reduction in the exchange risk of member countries' exporters.

EXECUTIVE MBA

An executive MBA (EMBA) blends some of the elements of part-time, modular and consortium programmes. Participants' courses are paid for by their companies, and the programmes are usually made up of fully sponsored executives with considerable work experience. Classes are typically held on Fridays and Saturdays and there are often large modules of residential work as well as international field trips. In return for high fees, the programmes draw on the schools' best teachers. A highly regarded EMBA can carry more prestige than an ordinary MBA. But critics say that EMBAS are not really MBAS at all but merely EXECUTIVE PROGRAMMES with a different title.

EXECUTIVE PROGRAMME

A training course at a BUSINESS SCHOOL designed for mature executives. Unlike the MBA, these short courses (lasting anything from a few days to a few months) do not provide participants with a qualification. Some of them (like Harvard's short course) have, however, gained considerable prestige in their own right. At some business schools the revenue from executive programmes accounts for well over half their income.

EXIT ROUTE

The route via which investors (especially venture capitalists) eventually realise the gain on their investment. There are a number of different exit routes for such investors. For example, their company may go public, thereby enabling them to sell their shares on a stockmarket; or there may be a sale for cash to a larger group. It sometimes seems unseemly to hear financiers talk of exit routes before anything has been entered into.

EXPATRIATE

A manager or skilled worker who is a foreigner in

the country where he or she is working and living. Strictly speaking, an expatriate is someone who is sent abroad by his or her employer for a comparatively short term. But this definition has been stretched to suit modern times. Expatriates nowadays may well be employed by the local subsidiary of the company that sent them, or indeed by a local company itself, for life. Expatriates who are sent to live in unappealing places expect to get a number of generous perks to compensate; for example, regular free trips back home, school fees for their children and various cost-of-living allowances. In general, the less pleasant the destination, the more perks the employee expects.

Experience curve

Part of the reason that unit costs decline as cumulative production increases; the effect of workers getting better at their jobs, manufacturing processes being improved, and support services beginning to function smoothly. The theory implies that the competitor who expands production CAPACITY fastest will achieve a cost advantage that will lead to industry dominance. First observed in manufacturing industries as the LEARNING CURVE, the concept was broadened beyond the ASSEMBLY LINE by Bruce Henderson, founder of the BOSTON CONSULTING GROUP. The idea helped fuel BCG's phenomenal growth in the 1970s.

Export finance

A loan granted to exporters to bridge the gap between the time that they ship their goods to a customer and the time they receive payment for them. With large capital goods, this bridge sometimes has to stretch as far as a couple of years.

Externalities

The incidental effects on others of a person's or a company's behaviour. These effects may be beneficial (as when somebody's newly painted house enhances a whole neighbourhood) or they may be damaging (as when customers discard all their litter in the streets surrounding a takeaway hamburger restaurant). The issue about externalities is: who pays for them? The whole neighbourhood does not make a contribution towards the one cleanly painted house in its midst.

Concern about industrial spoiling of the environment has brought the issue of externalities more into the corporate arena. Who is to pay for cleaning up industrial pollution in our rivers? Many countries pay lip service to the principle that the polluter pays. But the small fines imposed on the guilty show how ineffective this can be in practice.

Factor analysis

A statistical procedure in which a large number of variables (quantities that vary) are reduced to a manageable amount by finding clusters of them (called factors) that are interrelated. Factor analysis has been useful in analysing human personality. Clusters of different human variables ("all fat people are jolly") have led to the diagnosis of different personality types, such as manic-depressive and so on. Such analysis can be useful in deciding where to place people within the structure of an organisation.

Factor cost

A pure unsullied sort of cost that measures the price paid for the FACTORS OF PRODUCTION (land, labour and capital), that is, rent for land, wages for labour, and interest or dividends for capital. Added together these prices give the total factor cost of an article. This differs from the full cost, for it excludes any subsidies received for production, and it ignores any taxes paid during production or imposed on consumption (like VAT).

Gross domestic product, the measure of a country's output, is calculated either according to the market VALUE of all the goods and services produced by the country, or (by adding back subsidies and subtracting taxes) according to the factor cost of all those goods and services.

Factoring

The handing over to another organisation (usually a financial institution) of the responsibility for collecting a company's outstanding invoices – for a fee. In effect, OUTSOURCING the management of the cash ledger. There are two principal reasons for factoring.

- The company is too small for it to be efficient to run its own sales ledger. In this case, the factor will be paid a fee and will do everything from raising an invoice to chasing poor payers.
- The company is in need of cash and wants

to accelerate payments that are due. In this case, the factor buys the company's unpaid invoices at a discount and then sets about collecting the monies itself. This is a one-off operation, and the factor's fee is anything that it can collect above the discounted amount that it paid for the invoices.

In this second type of factoring (sometimes known as invoice discounting) the company may not wish it to be known that it has sold its invoices (and is therefore in need of cash). In such cases the factor may continue to send out claims for payment in the company's name.

FACTORS OF PRODUCTION

The fundamental elements (of land, labour and capital) that are required for the production and creation of economic wealth. (See also ENTREPRENEUR and FACTOR COST.)

FAMILY FIRM

The industrial wealth of all developed countries is built on the family business. Quoted companies as big, as old and as widely owned as Wal-Mart Stores, Barclays Bank and Fiat are still to a greater or lesser extent influenced by the offspring of the families that founded them. The heart of the vibrant small business sector is the family firm, and the urge to build up a business "for the children" seems to be no less strong now than it was 100 years ago.

The growth of stockmarkets around the world has accelerated the evolution of companies from tightly held, family-run businesses into widely held and professionally managed corporations. Usually, the family seeks to retain a controlling holding when they float their business, but this is often whittled away as family members sell shares, or their holdings are diluted by new share issues.

Family firms raise a number of special issues.

- The succession question. Which cousin is next in line?

- High-quality non-family managers. Do they have to be owners as well?
- DIRECTORS from outside the family. Do we want them or not?
- Growth tomorrow versus wealth today. Is this an acceptable dividend policy?

FAST-MOVING CONSUMER GOODS

See FMCG.

HENRI FAYOL

A Frenchman whose 19th-century ideas on management were highly influential in the early decades of the 20th century. Born in 1841, Fayol spent nearly all his working life with a French coal-mining company. He started as an engineer and ended up as managing DIRECTOR for 30 years, turning the company from near disaster into a model of industrial success.

His thinking was based on what became known as functionalism, a theory of organisation with a number of elements that were revolutionary at the time. These included the preparation of long-term plans of action, the regular production of management accounts, regular meetings of departmental heads, and the drawing up of organisation charts that obeyed the two unities: unity of command (one boss for every employee) and unity of direction (one boss and one plan for each business activity).

Fayol has been criticised for oversimplification arising from the nature of his own one-product, unsophisticated, near-monopoly business. Yet Fayol himself recognised that managers need to be flexible. "Rarely do we apply the same principle twice in identical situations," he once said.

FEASIBILITY STUDY

An analysis of how a new product will be manufactured technically, how it will be sold, and whether it is likely to make a profit. A feasibility study is more concerned with whether something is practically possible than a BUSINESS PLAN. A business plan is a more detailed examination of the financial background to a proposal; that is, whether the product in a favourable feasibility study can be designed to give the sort of financial returns that potential investors require.

FIFO

Short for first in, first out, a method of valuing INVENTORY for accounting purposes. A company has a sizeable stock of identical inputs to be used in production. They have been purchased at different times and at different prices. Are the most recent or the oldest purchases being used up first? Since they are identical, you cannot tell merely by looking at them. FIFO assumes that the oldest (probably those bought at the lowest price) are used up first, and is the opposite of LIFO.

FILO (first in, last out) is not a method of valuing stock; it is a description of the daily arrival and departure of the perfect boss.

FINANCIAL ENGINEERING

The manipulation of a company's finances in order to improve their appearance. Thus a company might find that it is able to raise long-term funds from one source (a bank or the stock-market, for instance) and, with those funds, is able to pay off pressing short-term creditors.

FIRST MOVER

The first company to take advantage of a new business opportunity. There are advantages to being a first mover – for a while, until others catch up, you have considerable autonomy in your pricing policy. But there are disadvantages too. You make more mistakes, mistakes that others can learn from and thus save themselves an expense that you have had to incur.

FLEXIBLE MANUFACTURING

A manufacturing system that can be cheaply and rapidly switched from making product A to making product B as and when market demand dictates. It is particularly well suited to products that have a strong seasonal demand, or to products that are susceptible to changing tastes and fashion.

Floating-rate note
A debt instrument on which the interest rate is adjusted periodically to take account of changing market conditions. The interest rate on floating-rate notes is often expressed with reference to some variable base point, frequently the London interbank offered rate (LIBOR). LIBOR is a variable rate which banks in London offer to pay to each other for the use of each other's foreign currency deposits.

Flow of funds
The amount of cash that is flowing through a business. A funds-flow statement, known in the UK as the statement of sources and applications of funds, used to be one of the main financial statements appearing in companies' annual reports. Its drawback was that it merely showed the changes taking place in the interval between two BALANCE SHEETS. It did not provide the additional information necessary to assess whether the flow of funds through the business was sufficient to enable the company to meet its obligations as and when they fell due. Since the late 1980s (in the United States) and early 1990s (in the UK) the funds-flow statement has been replaced by the CASHFLOW STATEMENT.

FMCG
Short for for fast-moving consumer goods, things like foodstuffs, toothpaste, and so on, that do not stay on shop shelves for long. The MARKETING of FMCGS requires special skills, which companies like Unilever and Procter & Gamble have in abundance.

Focus group
A group of people brought together by market researchers to discuss a particular product or service. Interaction between the participants is encouraged and the discussion is allowed to range widely. Focus groups are most commonly used

for new products, either immediately before or just after they are launched.

MARY PARKER FOLLETT

The first woman (described by one fan as a "gaunt Bostonian lady") to exert great influence on the study of management. Follett's first book (with the unlikely title of *The Speaker of the House of Representatives*) was published in 1898 and was firmly based on her origins as a political scientist. But it had clear relevance to management, being a study of how effective particular speakers had been as leaders of the house, and why.

Follett's subsequent writing was a reaction to the mechanistic ideas of FREDERICK TAYLOR and of scientific management. She saw workers as fallible human beings, not as sophisticated machines. The skill of management was to bring these human beings together into groups, and to understand what could make them operate successfully.

Management, not bankers nor stockbrokers, is the fundamental element in industry. It is good management that draws credit, that draws workers, that draws customers ... Management is the permanent function of business.

Mary Parker Follett

FORECASTING

No business can go far without making some guesses about what will happen in the future. These may be guesses about the general economy, about a company's specific markets, or about the supply and price of the raw materials that the company uses. Most forecasts are based partly on extrapolations from past experience. Since the past is never repeated, the forecast will almost certainly be wrong. A forecast (of something like PROFIT) that is based on a lot of other forecasts will therefore almost certainly be hugely wrong. Yet investors continue to be hugely surprised when companies' formal profit forecasts are not achieved.

Gilbert Heebner, an American economist, has drawn up a useful list of seven laws to take into account when forecasting (or when considering other people's forecasts).

- The future is not random; but history does not repeat itself exactly either.
- From time to time major (and usually unpredictable) shocks throw an economy off course.
- The consensus of economists' forecasts is more often right than wrong.
- Sticking for too long to one economic theory can be dangerous to your health as a forecaster.
- Economic forces work relentlessly, but on an uncertain timetable. So, many forecasts may be correct in all but their timing.
- Abnormalities are always significant.
- The road is more important than the inn: there is more to be learnt from the way the forecast is arrived at than from the forecast itself.

FRANCHISE

A popular way for a manufacturer or service company to distribute its goods or services widely without making all the required capital investment by itself. Some famous franchise operations include McDonald's restaurants and Benetton clothes shops. A franchisor usually gives a licence to a franchisee for a certain fee, which is frequently based on the franchisee's turnover. The licence gives the franchisee the exclusive right to sell the franchisor's goods or services in a particular area. In return, the franchisee has to meet certain standards demanded by the franchisor, and also has to buy supplies exclusively from the franchisor. Luciano Benetton says he gives franchises not necessarily to people with merchandising experience, but to people with "the right spirit".

FRN

See FLOATING-RATE NOTE.

FUNCTION

Most companies are structured in such a way that specific functions are combined into a single department or division (for example, MARKETING, design, R&D, and so on). Within each function the lines of responsibility go upwards, ending eventually on the shoulders of the chief executive.

If adequate lines of communication across the organisation and between different functions are not established then efficiency and responsiveness is reduced. For example, the full marketing potential of the findings of the R&D department may never be realised if the two functions rarely communicate.

In recent years companies have been switching their organisational structure from a focus on functions to a focus on PROCESSES. In many cases this was brought about as part of an exercise in BUSINESS PROCESS RE-ENGINEERING.

FUTURES

Contracts between parties who have different views of how things will turn out. Such contracts were first used in agricultural commodity markets where a farmer of, say, pork bellies sold his produce forward (that is, before it was fully grown) to a speculator. The speculator was betting that the price of pork bellies would be at such a level that he could sell them (when he eventually took possession) at a profit. Futures markets need these two types of investors: hedgers (such as the farmer) and speculators. Hedgers want to play safe; speculators want to take a risk.

From agricultural commodity markets, futures spread to financial markets, first to the foreign exchange markets, then to bond and stock markets. Secondary markets in futures were then developed to enable contracts to be bought and sold, and to give liquidity to the primary market.

In futures markets the three main financial

centres (corresponding to the world's three main time zones) – Tokyo in East Asia, London in Europe, and New York in the United States – have not had business all their own way. Futures markets in Singapore in East Asia, Paris in Europe and Chicago in the United States are all providing serious competition to the traditional financial capitals of those regions.

GANTT CHART

A type of chart named after Henry L. Gantt, an American who worked with FREDERICK TAYLOR. The charts became popular during the first world war as a tool to help plan wartime production. Managers continued to use them for many decades thereafter.

Gantt charts plot time along one axis and different tasks along the other. Each task is represented by a solid bar, which stretches across the time that it takes to be performed. Such simplistic devices have been largely superseded by the introduction of computerised methods of planning and monitoring production.

GAP ANALYSIS

A MARKETING technique for identifying gaps in a market that a company might be able to exploit. These gaps may lie in the shortcomings of existing products in the market, or in sets of neglected consumers, or in opportunities for PRODUCT DEVELOPMENT arising from new technology. The process of analysis consists of looking at the qualities of existing products and comparing them with all the qualities that a consumer might want in such a product.

The expression "gap analysis" is also sometimes used to refer to an examination of the difference between a target and a forecast, or between a forecast and an actual outcome.

GEARING

The ratio between a company's debt and its equity, known in the United States as leverage. The significant thing about gearing is what it says about two diverse forms of corporate finance. The cost of debt, for example, is a fixed cost (interest payments), but the cost of equity (dividends) is not. These differences have a material effect on corporate STRATEGY. Debt facilities are more easily and swiftly arranged, and hence are suitable for making the quick moves needed to seize brief market opportunities. Equity is more long-term, more stable and less demanding of instant returns.

Frank Gilbreth

An American building contractor who developed the ideas of FREDERICK TAYLOR, adding a psychological dimension to Taylor's automatism. Gilbreth was concerned with eliminating all unnecessary motion in order to find the best way to do manual work, and he pioneered the use of the camera to help him examine human behaviour. "Eliminating unnecessary distances that workers' hands and arms must travel will eliminate miles of motions per man in a working day," he wrote. In this way he improved the PRODUCTIVITY of his bricklayers enormously.

When Gilbreth died in 1924 his wife Lilian, an industrial psychologist, took up his work and travelled the world to promote his ideas. She died in 1972 at the ripe old age of 94, having found time to give birth to 12 children.

Glass ceiling

A phrase taken from the title of a 1988 book, *Shattering the Glass Ceiling* (written by Marilyn Davidson and Cary Cooper). It refers to the invisible barriers that prevent women from climbing to the top of the management ladder. In the European Union as a whole, women make up almost 40% of the workforce. Yet less than 2% of senior managers are women. Even in Scandinavia, where equal opportunities are widely assumed to be greatest, less than 10% of all management jobs are filled by women.

With the labour shortage that the demographic squeeze will bring to much of Europe, countries are keen to find ways in which they can break through the glass ceiling and make better managerial use of this underdeveloped two-fifths of their workforce.

Common reasons cited for the glass ceiling include the following.

- The pipeline. Senior managers take 20–25 years to reach the top of their careers. Women have not been managers in significant numbers for that long; in other

words, they are in the pipeline, but have not yet emerged at the top.
- Lack of broad-based experience. Women often choose (and are chosen for) jobs in support services. They get little opportunity to work in line management.
- The family. During their main childbearing years, between 25 and 34, women's job aspirations decline dramatically.
- A hostile corporate environment. In general, like will promote like. Since most bosses are men, they usually replace themselves with men.

Behind all this is an assumption that every right-minded person wants to pursue their management career to its bitter end. The truth may be that there are a lot of men who would like to be free to choose to raise their children. For them, there may be glass floorboards preventing them from getting off the ladder altogether.

Globalisation

The phenomenon whereby the market for products and services is extended to cover the whole globe. From Tbilisi to Santiago consumers drink Coca-Cola, eat Nestlé chocolate and drive Ford cars. In the old days, each country had its own distinctive range of products and services.

Globalisation allows companies to reap massive ECONOMIES OF SCALE, but distribution and MARKETING become major challenges. There are a number of ways in which companies can pursue globalisation.

- Export their products from one or two domestic production facilities. This is what companies like Gillette do, and what Japanese car manufacturers used to do in the 1980s. It is a STRATEGY that enables them to gain enormous economies of scale.
- Set up a series of franchises with local operators around the globe. This is particularly suitable where a key element in

the formula is service, which can be supplied well only by people who understand the local culture. Companies like the Hertz car-hire group and McDonald's restaurants have gone global in this way.

- Set up manufacturing operations in many different countries, each with its own distribution and marketing facilities. This was a popular route for the early MULTINATIONALS like Shell and Unilever, but it is an expensive and high-risk one.

GMAT

The Graduate Management Admission Test (GMAT) is used by many business schools as a basic guide to an applicant's suitability for an MBA course. The test is administered as a computer-adaptive test (known as GMAT CAT) in hundreds of locations throughout the world. A paper-based GMAT is offered twice a year where the network of computer-based testing sites is not yet available.

The GMAT CAT includes verbal, quantitative and analytical written questions. The verbal and quantitative sections are computer adaptive, but the analytical written questions are not. The GMAT CAT is offered three weeks a month, six days a week, throughout the year at more than 400 computer-based testing centres in North America and selected cities around the world. Masochists can take the test once every calendar month.

The Educational Testing Service (PO Box 6108, Princeton, NJ 08541, US) supplies registration forms and the *GMAT Bulletin of Information*, which lists test centres and some sample questions. The website at www.gmat.org has details of the test, sample questions and other useful information. The *Official Guide to GMAT Review* contains over 700 sample questions, a complete test and a guide to the different question sections. There is also some software that reproduces CAT-style questions on PCS.

Going concern

An accounting concept. When carrying out an

AUDIT, auditors assume that the companies whose accounts they are checking are going to continue in business for some time (as a going concern). If they do not make that assumption, the method of valuing the companies' ASSETS changes radically. A company that is not a going concern is one that is about to go out of business. Its assets are worth only what can be obtained for them in a "fire" sale.

Goodwill

The VALUE in a business that cannot be kicked; the amount that somebody is prepared to pay for the business over and above a strict valuation of its ASSETS. This premium may arise because the company has some obvious intangible advantage: a great research team, famous BRANDS, and so on. Or it may arise because a competitor is prepared to pay extra in order to eliminate some of its competition.

Growth

The aim of most companies is to grow. It is virtually impossible to stay still, and there is little credit to be gained from shrinking, which is still seen as the start of the slippery slope to corporate failure. There are three basic ways in which a company can grow:

- organically, by increasing its existing business through the use of its own internal resources;
- by MERGERS AND ACQUISITIONS, buying extra business from elsewhere;
- by the currently popular route of ALLIANCES.

Growth share matrix

A concept invented by a firm of consultants, the BOSTON CONSULTING GROUP, in the 1960s, and often known as the Boston boxes. The growth share matrix provides a framework for thinking about the STRATEGY of different companies within a large group by defining them along two axes: their MARKET SHARE and the GROWTH rate of the sector they are in.

The matrix divides into four sections, which BCG called CASH COWS (the low-growth, high-share businesses), dogs (the low-growth, low-share businesses), stars (the high-growth, high-share businesses) and question marks (the high-growth, low-share businesses). Each section requires a different sort of strategic treatment.

The growth share matrix proved to be one of the most popular strategic tools ever created. But its assumption that high market share gives high profitability has been questioned. As a result of its shortcomings, some companies have attempted to refine the basic matrix, adding squares and changing the axes.

HACKER

A word that has come to be used to refer to computer experts who use their programming skills to break into other people's systems and cause electronic damage. The word was originally intended to refer to computer experts who used their skills to build and create new things within IT, people who hacked their way through the electronic undergrowth in order to solve specific problems.

MICHAEL HAMMER

A professor of computer science at the Massachusetts Institute of Technology (MIT), who in the early 1990s published an article in the *Harvard Business Review* that first propounded the idea of BUSINESS PROCESS RE-ENGINEERING. He subsequently wrote a book on the subject that became a bestseller and laid down the ground rules for what transpired to be one of the most compelling management ideas of the 1990s. Hammer also became a focus for the backlash, a tirade of hostility against the corporate DOWNSIZING and management lay-offs that came to be seen as the inevitable accompaniment of all corporate re-engineering.

HAND-OFF

The transfer of work from one person or department to another. Hand-offs are notorious sources of error and delay, so OPERATIONAL RESEARCH experts go to great lengths to minimise the number of hand-offs when they are designing production processes and so on.

CHARLES HANDY

An unconventional British writer on management who worked for the Shell oil company for many years before becoming a professor at the London Business School. Management, he maintains, is "a soft theory area. It is not precise. I have a great dislike for people who are looking for a hard law for management". As a Shell executive in Borneo, Handy cast aside BUSINESS SCHOOL lessons that taught him that the purpose of a company is to "maximise medium-term earnings per share". That idea, he said, was "very remote, very long-term, very intellectual, very unreal". As a manager he found "concepts and ideas abounding", but too often also found "ponderous confirmation of the obvious, and weighty investigation of trivia".

Hawthorne effect

This is the most famous finding of what is probably the most famous industrial experiment of all time. The experiment started in 1927 at the Western Electric Company's Hawthorne factory in Chicago, and continued for a decade or so thereafter. It involved some 20,000 workers and almost 100 investigators from Harvard, led by an Australian social psychologist called Elton Mayo. The Hawthorne effect was the finding that factory workers worked harder when the level of the lighting in their plant was increased. Then they worked harder again when the level of lighting was decreased. It was not the physical conditions themselves that were motivating them, but the fact that somebody somewhere was concerned about their welfare and found the time to talk to them about it.

Headhunter

A person who specialises in finding and recruiting senior managers and professional staff on behalf of others. This can be an extremely rewarding business; headhunters often take up to one-third of the first year's pay of the "heads" that they place. They do well in industries where particular skills are in short supply; for example, in the finance industry on Wall Street and in the City of London during boom times, when sometimes they recruit whole teams of financial specialists, poaching them from one firm and persuading them to join another. Headhunting agencies are also known as executive search firms.

Hedging

The process of shifting the risk of future price changes from one party to another. Any company that has to make plans on the basis of anticipated future prices (of raw materials or foreign exchange, for example) must consider hedging. This takes place on a growing number of sophisticated futures markets, a place where risk-averse businesses can hand over their risks to risk-loving speculators.

HERFINDAHL INDEX

A measure of the CONCENTRATION of an industry or industry sector, a figure frequently used by ANTITRUST authorities to help them judge whether deals that will increase concentration should be allowed to go ahead. The index takes the square of the MARKET SHARE of each firm in an industry (expressed as a fraction) and adds them together. The closer that sum comes to 1, the more dominant is the industry leader. (An index of 1 means that a single firm has a 100% market share.)

FREDERICK HERZBERG

An American psychologist, who in 1968 wrote "One More Time: How Do You Motivate Employees?", the best-selling article that the *Harvard Business Review* has ever published. Herzberg tries to reconcile the human and economic factors within industry, "the dominant institution in the world".

> *Our love affair with numbers is the root cause of the passionlessness of the 1980s. Numbers numb our feelings for what is being counted and lead to the adoration of the economies of scale. Passion is in feeling the quality of experience, not in trying to measure it.*
>
> Frederick Hertzberg

GEERT HOFSTEDE

The man who is considered to be the father of cross-cultural management – a suitable subject for a multilingual, multicultural Dutchman. Most of the work on cross-cultural management starts with Hofstede's study into the factors that make up the culture of employees in different countries. He found four dimensions along which there were significant cultural differences between people of different nationalities.

- Collectivism/individualism.
- Power distance. How comfortable people are with inequalities in the distribution of power.
- Uncertainty avoidance.
- Femininity/masculinity. He maintains that Japan's is a masculine culture and Sweden's a feminine one.

The nature of management skills is such that they are culturally specific: a management technique or philosophy that is appropriate in one national culture is not necessarily appropriate in another.

Geert Hofstede

HORIZONTAL INTEGRATION

The merger of organisations in the same (or similar) businesses, as opposed to VERTICAL INTEGRATION. Thyssen buying Krupp is an example of horizontal integration; General Motors buying Electronic Data Systems is not. Horizontal integration is more likely to make ANTITRUST authorities hot under the collar.

HOT-DESKING

The practice of allocating offices and desks to employees as and when they are needed. With hot-desking, no one individual has a specific desk or office that they can call their own. They book a desk (and its attendant PC) in advance and for a particular time. The next day someone else may use the same desk and PC.

HUMAN RESOURCE MANAGEMENT

A common expression for all aspects of management dealing with people. It encompasses more than the older expression, personnel management. Whereas personnel management is involved only with the nitty-gritty of employees' lives (their pensions, company cars, health check-ups, and so on), human resource management (HRM) covers wider policy issues such as training, recruitment and relocation. MICHAEL PORTER says "every activity (in industry) involves human resources, so human resource management spans the whole VALUE CHAIN". It is one of only three activities to do so, the other two being technological development and procurement.

HURDLE RATE

The RATE OF RETURN required for a project to be worthwhile; that is, a higher rate of return than would have been obtained by leaving the capital required by the project idle in a bank. The expected rate of return is calculated by using DISCOUNTED CASHFLOW techniques.

Income statement
See PROFIT AND LOSS ACCOUNT.

Incremental analysis
The process of analysing the costs and benefits to a company of developing a product or service on the back of its existing overheads. Companies that want to develop new products in order to use up spare production CAPACITY, or to make use of advantageous access to a distribution NETWORK, will cost the new products using analysis in which some of the major costs are incremental.

Incremental business is often undertaken with the aim of making a positive contribution to a loss-making operation. But there is no point doing business that makes an incremental profit if the underlying business is making a larger than incremental loss.

Industrial policy
The nature and extent of government intervention in a country's industry. This varies greatly from country to country. Most countries have a policy of encouraging investment in industry, and they set about it with a host of investment grants and tax incentives. Industrial policy is often linked with regional policy (trying to encourage industry to set up in particular depressed areas), or environmental policy (forcing, or giving incentives to, firms to cut down on their emission of noxious gases, for example).

In many free-market economies, competition policy has increasingly become the core of industrial policy as governments have accepted that free and fair competition is one of the best ways of ensuring long-term industrial growth.

Industrial relations
A term that has come to refer specifically to the relations between employees and unions on the one hand and management on the other. A proxy measure for the state of industrial relations in a country is the number of working days lost through strikes.

Inflation accounting

The attempt to create accounts that will get around the problem of rising prices, that is, of inflation. It disturbs accountants that something bought by a company for $100 at the beginning of a financial year can cost $120 by the end of that year if inflation is 20%. What if that something is sold at the end of the year for $115? Has the company made a profit of $15 or a loss of $5?

In the 1970s there was an enthusiastic search for a method of accounting for inflation. It was led by the accounting authorities in the UK and the United States, whose rules often set standards for the rest of the world. But nobody found a satisfactory method, so in 1983 the search was abandoned, just at the time when inflation in the UK and the United States conveniently dropped almost out of sight.

It was still raging in other parts of the world, however, where accountants were left to fend for themselves. In Turkey, where inflation was persistently over 50% a year throughout the 1990s, the absence of rules on inflation accounting enabled companies like Polly Peck to declare huge profits that were mostly an accounting mirage.

Information technology

The combination of computers and telecommunications and the remarkable things that they can achieve together, more commonly known by the simple abbreviation IT. IT has revolutionised the way in which companies organise themselves. By making information potentially available to anybody anywhere, it has reduced the need for the type of manager whose job was essentially to push information up and down the organisation.

Initial public offering

A company's first offering of shares to the general public, a time when a company's founders turn the VALUE that their company has created into cash in their bank accounts. This makes it the ultimate aim of most ENTREPRENEURS and new businesses. For some entrepreneurs, however, the public scrutiny that comes with a public offering is more than they can stomach. Richard Branson, for instance, took his Virgin group public with an initial public offering (IPO) and then turned it back into a private company.

Business is not the art of having new ideas all the time. It is the art of using your new ideas sparingly, and in the right dosage, at the right moment.
Georges Doriot, Harvard Business School

INNOVATION
A critical part of the business process: the addition of new elements to products or services, or to the methods of producing them. Innovation is not the creation of an entirely new product – that is invention, which is comparatively rare. It is, rather, the continuous process of adding to and improving a product so as to gain an edge over its competitors (see also CONTINUOUS IMPROVEMENT). Francis Bacon, an Elizabethan poet, was as interested in the process of innovation as any of today's management gurus. "He that will not apply new remedies must expect new evils," he wrote. "For time is the greatest innovator."

Innovation is 1% inspiration and 99% perspiration.
Thomas Edison

INSTITUTIONAL INVESTOR
An institution that gathers the savings of others and invests them on their behalf. In this way, the institution brings the powers of scale to the capital markets. Typical institutional investors include pension funds, insurance companies and investment trusts.

INTANGIBLE ASSETS
ASSETS that cannot be kicked. An accounting term used to refer to things like GOODWILL, PATENTS,

BRAND names and trademarks, which have a VALUE even though they are (literally) intangible. Although nobody denies that these things are worth something, problems arise when they try to decide how much.

INTELLECTUAL PROPERTY

Ideas, inventions, designs or books that belong to their creator. Although intellectual property can be protected by PATENTS, registered trademarks and copyright law, it is particularly vulnerable to theft.

Intellectual property has become one of the most contentious areas of international trade. It has been estimated that American companies alone lose $40 billion–50 billion a year from the unauthorised use of technology by foreign manufacturers. In a landmark judgment in a New Jersey court in 1992, an American computer company, Honeywell, was awarded $96m compensation for technology stolen by a Japanese camera company, Minolta. From 1984 Honeywell inventions had been used by Minolta in its autofocus and automatic lens shutter cameras, and not a yen was paid to Honeywell in royalties. The case highlighted calls for international rules and procedures to protect intellectual property.

INTERNAL RATE OF RETURN

The internal rate of return (IRR) is the interest rate at which the discounted future CASHFLOW from a project exactly equals the investment in the project. In general, this must be higher than the MARGINAL COST of capital for it to be worth going ahead with the project.

INTERNET

A worldwide communications network linking millions of computers via telephone lines. Originally set up by American academic and defence establishments, the net is growing at a phenomenal rate, helped by the development of the WORLD WIDE WEB, a graphical interface allowing sound and pictures to be transmitted, and the creation of browser software, allowing access to the large (but chaotically organised) quantity of information on the Internet.

INTRANET

A network of computer systems with restricted access, unlike the INTERNET, where access is unlimited. Intranets (formerly known as file servers) are popular within single organisations. Often set up with sites in different locations, they are used as a means of facilitating communication and the transfer of knowledge between employees of the organisation.

INTRAPRENEURSHIP

A term that combines the idea of entrepreneurship with *intra* (the Latin for inside or within). It means the PROMOTION of the qualities of the ENTREPRENEUR inside a big corporation. The idea became popular with the realisation that small entrepreneurial firms are nimble and quick to change, whereas large companies are more like dinosaurs, in danger of extinction because their brains are too small for their bodies.

INVENTORY

The American expression for what the British call STOCK-IN-TRADE. The word inventory avoids confusion between stocks (the usual abbreviation for stock-in-trade) and stocks (as in stocks and shares).

INVESTOR RELATIONS

The growing business of keeping a company's shareholders happy and informed, and of cultivating other potential investors who might in time become shareholders. It is part of a general adjustment in corporations' perceptions of themselves as market-driven organisations that operate in labour markets, consumer markets and financial markets.

INVISIBLES

Invisible trade, that is, exports and imports that

you cannot drop on a stevedore. Invisibles include things like insurance, interest payments, or tourists' stays in hotel rooms. Some countries have large surpluses of invisibles. They are usually the countries (like the UK and the United States) that have large deficits on visibles (that is, manufactured goods).

IPO
See INITIAL PUBLIC OFFERING.

IRR
See INTERNAL RATE OF RETURN.

IT
See INFORMATION TECHNOLOGY.

JIT

See JUST-IN-TIME.

JOBBING

A system of production used when the quantity of goods to be produced is too small to justify either BATCH production or MASS PRODUCTION. Jobbing is often found in the engineering industry where orders (for machine tools, for instance) are made in small numbers. Such production needs particularly careful planning, each product requiring slightly different operations in a different sequence. With jobbing it is difficult to forecast production times.

JOINT VENTURE

A business venture entered into jointly by two or more partners. Companies favour joint ventures when they are exploring a new market or a new geographical region. Their main aim is to share the risk, but it helps if one of the partners has some local or specialised knowledge of the market to be explored. Joint ventures have become popular as more and more companies seek to enter new markets abroad.

Many joint ventures split up after a while, with the partners deciding to go their separate ways. But some joint ventures have a long and impressive track record. Unilever, for example, the Anglo-Dutch giant, is the result of a century-old joint venture between Lever Brothers of the UK and J. Van den Bergh of the Netherlands.

JUNK BOND

The emotionally charged name for a certain sort of debt security that was popular in the 1980s. Forever associated with a now defunct investment bank, Drexel Burnham Lambert, and its criminal chief junk-bond dealer, Michael Milken, junk bonds have come to smell worse than junk.

Their image is not entirely justified. Technically, a junk bond is no more than a bond issued by an organisation in the United States that has less than a certain rating from the principal credit-rating agencies. Many American pension funds and insurance companies are strictly limited in the number of bonds with a junk rating that they can buy.

In the mid-1980s fewer than 1,000 companies merited higher than a junk rating. This left some 20,000 American companies with ASSETS of over $25m and virtually no access to the bond market, until Drexel came along and created a market for them. The problem with junk bonds was that they could be issued by small companies from America's heartlands, where the risk was small, or they could be the bonds of once high-flying firms that were in a steep dive towards bankruptcy. Drexel dealt in both.

J.J. Juran

The second most famous American quality management guru after W. EDWARDS DEMING. Juran's writing style is more ponderous and his method more systematic, but his influence on the Japanese has probably been as great as Deming's. His methods are now perpetuated through the Juran Institute in Connecticut.

Just-in-time

A Japanese management system based on the principle that nothing should arrive for processing within a manufacturing company until the moment that it is actually needed. Just-in-time (JIT) relies heavily on sophisticated LOGISTICS programs, but it can make enormous savings by reducing dramatically the need to hold INVENTORY. The crucial skill is to make sure that JIT doesn't become JTL, or just-too-late.

KAIZEN

See CONTINUOUS IMPROVEMENT.

KANBAN

The cards that constitute orders for parts in the famous JUST-IN-TIME production system devised by Japan's Toyota motor company. When a team working on one part of the Toyota manufacturing process needs parts from another team, it merely sends them the empty parts tray together with the tray's *kanban*. This constitutes a production order to the second team. The demand for parts is thus filtered backwards throughout the manufacturing process.

ROSABETH MOSS KANTER

One of the most influential of the late 20th century generation of American business academics, Rosabeth Moss Kanter combined an academic career with a consultancy business that kept her in touch with the real world. This is a pattern of work favoured by other high-flying management academics such as MICHAEL PORTER and IGOR ANSOFF. Kanter's most famous book is *The Change Masters* in which she looks at the conditions necessary to encourage INNOVATION. She likes using literary metaphors to describe business, as do PETER DRUCKER, a Jane Austen fan, and WARREN BENNIS, a Tolstoy fan.

> *I think the game that best describes most businesses today is the croquet game in Alice in Wonderland. In that game nothing remains stable for very long. Everything is changing around the players. Alice goes to hit a ball, but her mallet is a flamingo. Just as she is about to hit the ball, the flamingo lifts its head and looks in another direction. That's just like technology and the tools we use. Just when employees have mastered them, they seem to change, requiring different learning and competence.*

(See also EMPOWERMENT.)

A.T. Kearney

A leading firm of consultants, specialising in LOGISTICS and SUPPLY CHAIN MANAGEMENT. Founded in 1946, A.T. Kearney joined forces with EDS, a global outsourcing company, in 1995. The firm was set up by Andrew Thomas Kearney, a MARKETING specialist who had been J.O. MCKINSEY's first partner in his eponymous firm in 1929. Tom Kearney's most famous quote was: "The world's work is done with imperfect men."

Keiretsu

A large group of Japanese financial and industrial companies that are interlinked by cross-shareholdings and by long-term commercial relationships. Once known as *zaibatsu*, the more modern name for these groups, *keiretsu*, means "headless combines". The most famous *keiretsu* include Mitsubishi, Sumitomo and Mitsui.

Japan's industrial success is sometimes attributed to the existence of the *keiretsu*. But some of the fastest-growing Japanese companies of the past few decades have been firms such as Toyota, Sony and Canon, none of which is part of a *keiretsu*.

Manfred Kets de Vries

A psychoanalyst who teaches at INSEAD, a leading European business school, Kets de Vries has had a powerful influence on many of the senior managers who have passed through the school's short courses. His speciality is corporate neurosis. He links much of the mindless management of big organisations with a clinical disorder known as alexithymia. The symptoms of this widespread disorder include an impoverished fantasy life, a paucity of inner emotional experience, a tendency to engage in stereotypical interpersonal behaviour and a speech pattern characterised by endless, trivial, repetitive details. Kets de Vries maintains that:

> *Big companies possess the kind of numbing quality which awakens dormant alexithymic*

tendencies in their employees. The climb to the executive suite is not enhanced by eccentric behaviour.

In other words, executives must fit, "and that does not make for the best and the brightest".

KEY PERFORMANCE INDICATOR
"You cannot MANAGE what you cannot measure," goes the old saying. But you cannot measure and monitor everything. Hence a company needs to select a few key indicators of performance, things it can measure and monitor and that stand as a good proxy for the company's overall performance. These indicators, which can be either financial or performance-based, are known as KPIS.

KNOW-HOW
A saleable technique or skill that has been developed by a company. For example, when JIT was first developed it was known as the Toyota manufacturing system. For a while, until other companies adopted the idea, JIT was a part of Toyota's know-how.

Know-how may be more tangibly attributed to products: the recipe for Sara Lee's Pecan Pie, for example, or the technique of semi-freezing prepared foods developed by Marks & Spencer. Once it is widely available and widely used, however, its VALUE diminishes. When everybody knows how, there is no know-how.

KNOWLEDGE MANAGEMENT
The way that an organisation obtains, disseminates within itself and uses information (knowledge). As the VALUE of information has become more widely appreciated, organisations have tried to make better use of the accumulated knowledge held by the people who work for them. This has required better knowledge management.

KNOWLEDGE WORKER
This is what every worker will have to become in the future if he or she wants to continue to have a

job. As arduous manual work is automated into history (or sidelined by the growth of IT-based businesses), the only thing of VALUE to organisations will be knowledge.

Philip Kotler

A leading expert on MARKETING and the author of a classic standard textbook, *Marketing Management.* Kotler has been a counterweight to the enthusiasm for GLOBALISATION, arguing that markets are becoming more fragmented, not less so.

Mass markets are becoming 'demassified'. They are dissolving into hundreds of micro-markets.
Philip Kotler

KPI

See KEY PERFORMANCE INDICATOR.

LAN

See LOCAL AREA NETWORK.

LATERAL THINKING

The main contribution to management thinking of EDWARD DE BONO: the idea that our thought processes must sometimes force themselves to move sideways rather than in a strict linear motion, up and down. From these lateral leaps come the great sparks of originality that make for successful businesses.

De Bono has said that there are five aspects to lateral thinking.

- Escaping from cliché and fixed patterns of response.
- Constant challenging of assumptions.
- Habitually coming up with alternatives.
- Seizing new ideas without thought for the consequences.
- Finding new angles from which to think about old subjects.

Lateral thinking turns up an idea.
Vertical thinking develops it.
Edward de Bono

LEADERSHIP

There are some basic human traits that are believed to mark those people who have the quality of leadership. These include vision, integrity and a willingness to take risks. Leaders are also persistent and will try anything to achieve their goals. They lead by instinct. Managers who are out of touch with their instincts are said to be unlikely to make good leaders. Some researchers believe that leaders are also more likely to have been the eldest or only child in their family, inner-directed rather than responsive to others.

WARREN BENNIS, one of the most widely read gurus on leadership, goes along with the inner-directed view, developing an idea put forward by David Riesman in a 1950s book called *The Lonely*

Crowd. In his book *On Becoming a Leader*, published in 1989, Bennis examined 28 subjects who he maintained were true leaders. He found that a surprisingly high number of them had had multiple careers, and they themselves believed that the multiplicity had helped them to become leaders. The typical leader is not a person who has spent 30 years climbing the ladder of the same organisation.

Multiplicity of experience also emerges as an important factor in other studies of leadership. David Norburn, a British academic who studied a large sample of chief executives, found:

> *The major unifying characteristic which distinguishes the chief executive is exposure to multiple experiences. In early childhood, the challenge of an urban cosmopolitan or colonial infrastructure. In education, cerebral development of a more general nature by an arts first degree (rather than narrower sciences). At the time of entry into occupation, rapid exposure to different functions, followed by international commercial exposure.*

Great leaders are always fanatically committed to their jobs. They do not suffer from the crippling need to be universally loved.

David Ogilvy

LEAN PRODUCTION

A term used to refer to the remarkable manufacturing techniques developed by the Japanese to reduce their production costs and make them competitive with their American and European rivals. In the early 1970s lean production enabled Toyota to sell forklift trucks at prices that were close to Western manufacturers' cost of materials. Moreover, the company did not seem to be DUMPING since its prices in Japan were more or less the same as its export prices. This competitive superiority on cost was the basis of Japan's rapid success in exporting manufactured goods.

LEARNING CURVE
The graph of knowledge over time, a slope that (normally) moves from the bottom left-hand corner to the top right-hand corner. "He's on a steep learning curve" refers to someone who is picking up new skills quickly.

LEARNING ORGANISATION
A concept developed by a behavioural psychologist, CHRIS ARGYRIS, which describes the company (or organisation) that "learns" as its employees learn. In the learning organisation, systems and methods are altered to take account of things learnt. Thus the organisation retains knowledge independent of its employees. In the words of a management guru, PETER SENGE, a learning organisation is "an organisation that is continually expanding its capacity to create its future".

LEVERAGE
See GEARING.

THEODORE LEVITT
Like PETER DRUCKER, Theodore Levitt arrived in the United States as a refugee from Nazi Germany. He became a professor of MARKETING at Harvard Business School and a forthright editor of the *Harvard Business Review*, by far the best academic journal on management. He was succeeded as editor by ROSABETH MOSS KANTER in March 1990.

"Marketing Myopia", Levitt's 1960 article in the *Harvard Business Review,* was one of the most popular ever to appear in the journal. It marked a shift towards the customer-conscious corporation that led eventually to the "excellence" philosophies of the 1980s. Levitt is perhaps now most famous for his popularisation of the idea of the global BRAND. Behind this lay a belief that almost anything could be turned into a Coca-Cola, a uniform product sold in exactly the same way in every market around the world.

LIABILITIES
Items that appear on the opposite side of a

balance sheet to ASSETS; what is owed by a business to its creditors. A company's assets minus its liabilities are equal to its net worth, the underlying VALUE belonging to its shareholders.

LICENSING

Selling (for a fee) the rights to market a product or service in another country. Licensing is a low-cost way to enter a foreign market, since most of the risks are borne by the licensee. It may involve relinquishing much of the PROFIT from that market, but it can also be a cheap way of ensuring that competitors do not have the market to themselves.

LIFETIME VALUE

The VALUE placed on an ASSET over the whole of its lifetime, but with reference to one asset in particular: a firm's customers. Modern MARKETING theory suggests that customers should be looked upon as lifetime assets with a lifetime value. They should not be valued solely on the basis of a single transaction, but on their potential as purchasers throughout their lifetime. Their expected future transactions can then be discounted to give a NET PRESENT VALUE to their stream of future purchases. Traditionally, customers stay with a single bank for the whole of their banking lifetime. Hence, for example, the profitability of their first purchase (of, perhaps, a student loan) should be viewed in the context of the many other transactions that are likely to follow.

LIFO

Short for last in, first out, the opposite of FIFO. A method of accounting for stocks that assumes the last stocks to be purchased are the first to be used in production. The later that stocks are bought the more expensive they usually are, so LIFO effectively increases a company's costs. Hence under LIFO companies have lower PROFITS than under FIFO. British companies prefer FIFO; continental European companies favour LIFO.

LIMITED LIABILITY

One of the great inventions of capitalism: the granting to a company by law of a limit to its liability. For a company limited by shares the maximum liability is the share capital, effectively the amount still unpaid on the shares. For a company limited by guarantee, the maximum liability is the amount that the members of the company have guaranteed to pay in the event of liquidation.

For companies to retain the privilege of limited liability they have to follow certain rules. They and their owners have to be registered with the relevant authorities, and they have to indicate clearly in their literature that they are limited in this way.

The consequence of limited liability is that every business has to live with the reality of bad and doubtful debts, the result of doing business with limited companies that overreach their limit. Without limited liability, however, every DIRECTOR or owner of a company would be personally liable for all of the company's debts. In such a situation few people would be prepared to start a new business, and we would probably still live in a world of small craftsmen and medieval guilds.

LINE MANAGEMENT

Managers who are primarily responsible for the actual production of a company's goods and services. This classification is an analogy with the military, where line duties are those in the front line of fighting and staff duties are those in support. In companies too, staff managers provide support services for line managers, such as planning, human resources and shipping. However, the distinction between line and staff jobs is increasingly artificial. There are today few line jobs that have no involvement with, say, planning or personnel.

LIQUIDATION

The process of making liquid a company's ASSETS with the intention of paying off its debts. The corporate equivalent of execution and burial. The tidying up of a company's affairs when it ceases to do business. This usually occurs because the company is unable to pay its debts, but it can occur because the company's owners have decided that it has achieved what it set out to do (when it is referred to as a voluntary winding-up).

The corporate undertaker (called the liquidator) is usually an accountant or a solicitor, but does not have to be. His or her main job is to ascertain the exact amount owed to the company's creditors, and then to sell the company's assets in order to pay back to the creditors as much as possible. Not all creditors are equal, however. Some have priority over others. Secured creditors are paid first, followed by preferential creditors like the liquidator and the tax collector. The rest follow, *pari passu*.

Local area network

Commonly known as a LAN. A computer NETWORK covering a small geographical area. All the PCS at a BUSINESS SCHOOL, for example, or in a government department or a company.

Logistics

One of those military terms that still hang around the language of management. Logistics was originally the science of moving and supplying troops in the army; now it is the science of moving and supplying troops in a company's workforce. For huge MULTINATIONALS, such as General Motors, Unilever and BP, it is a formidable task.

Loss leader

Goods or services that are sold at a loss to entice consumers into buying something else that makes the supplier a hefty profit. Loss leaders are common in supermarkets, where a well-known BRAND is sold at a rock-bottom price to persuade customers to come in and do all of their grocery shopping there. Such goods are often sold on a limited availability basis: "while stocks last" or "the first 50 customers only". The initiative for choosing loss leaders is taken by the retailer, and not all manufacturers are happy with the practice. Some have been known to withhold supplies from stores that have sold their products as loss leaders.

LOYALTY
The practice of purchasing the same BRAND over and over again. Consumers who make repeat purchases again and again are referred to as "loyals". The "disloyals" purchase once and then move on to another brand, perhaps returning to the original one at a future date.

M&A
See MERGERS AND ACQUISITIONS.

MANAGE
The use of the word predates the Industrial Revolution by several centuries. Its origin is the Italian word *manneggiare* (to handle), referring to the handling of horses: "Speak termes of mannage to thy bounding steed," as William Shakespeare put it. Today the word "manège" still means horsemanship.

By the time the term "management" had come into common parlance it had a hint of scheming and trickery about it, a connotation that Joseph Addison, a British essayist, intended when he wrote at the beginning of the 17th century that the Duke of Savoy "had great management with several ecclesiastics before he turned hermit". At about the same time as Addison was writing, the word "manager" was first being used to refer to someone who ran a business or institution.

MANAGEMENT BUY-OUT
The raising of large sums of money by a team of managers to buy the company they run. Those who provide the money use the company's ASSETS as collateral for the loans, or they acquire shares in the bought-out company. If all the money for the purchase is borrowed then the company is likely to be highly geared. If the money comes as VENTURE CAPITAL in return for shares, the managers will have accepted a lower stake in the company as the price for lower GEARING.

A variation on the management buy-out (MBO) is the less common management buy-in (MBI). In this case, a team of managers from outside the company buys it in order to run it.

MANAGEMENT BY EXCEPTION
A management philosophy: the policy of only looking closely at events that deviate significantly from an expected norm. So, for example, anything less than a 10% drop in a sales manager's record will not be programmed to ring alarm bells; or,

say, no creditors will be pestered until they are at least 60 days overdue.

Management by objectives
An employee-friendly management method popular in the 1960s. Its main principle is that employer and employee sit down together to agree on the objectives to be achieved by the employee. Progress towards these objectives is then monitored by both sides, supposedly in a mutually harmonious way.

Management consultant
An adviser whose aim is to help companies to identify management problems, to analyse them, to recommend solutions, and (when requested) to help in implementing those solutions. The management consulting business has grown enormously in recent years. This has led to calls for companies' own managers to do more of their own identifying, analysing and resolving.

The term management consultant is used to cover people carrying out a wide range of functions, but there are four main areas of business consultancy:

- IT, the fastest growing area;
- manufacturing;
- organisational effectiveness (including finance and MARKETING);
- corporate STRATEGY.

A consultant is a person who takes your money and annoys your employees while tirelessly searching for the best way to extend the consulting contract.
Scott Adams, *The Dilbert Principle*

Management development
A catch-all phrase referring to the teaching and nurturing of management skills (for example, teambuilding or negotiation) rather than the teaching of specific technical skills (like engineering or

accounting). Any systematic training of managers depends on having a clear knowledge of what managers need to do. There are eight functions that are generally agreed to be central to the job of managing:

- planning
- organising
- staffing
- supervising
- directing
- controlling
- co-ordinating
- innovating.

MARGINAL COST

The cost of producing one extra item. This is not the same as the AVERAGE COST of production. Marginal cost ignores the cost of the plant and equipment needed to produce the goods. When business is slack and a plant has considerable surplus CAPACITY, marginal cost is the lowest price that a manufacturer can charge for goods without actually incurring a loss.

The concept of prices and costs at the margin is a common one in economics and in business. For example, the marginal PRODUCTIVITY of capital is the annual return that is earned by adding one extra unit of capital to an investment. The marginal propensity to consume is that percentage of one extra unit of income that a consumer will choose to spend (rather than to save).

MARKET CAPITALISATION

The VALUE of a company according to a stockmarket; that is, the price of its shares times the number of shares in issue. Market capitalisation is often used as a yardstick for measuring the relative value of different companies. But as such it has certain shortcomings. It cannot, for example, take account of non-quoted companies or state-owned industries (a significant chunk in many countries), and it always exaggerates the size of Japanese companies. Their stockmarket prices are determined by influences that are different from those in the West.

Market leader
The product or service that sells the most compared with the other products or services in its industrial segment. Microsoft, for instance, is the market leader in the market for PC operating systems. Many companies believe that they should not be in markets where their products are not either the market leader or among the leading two or three in the segment.

Market penetration
The percentage of all the potential customers for a product or service who have at some time purchased that product or service. A company seeking to increase its market penetration needs to persuade more consumers to try its products. To do this it has to use MARKETING techniques such as ADVERTISING, broader distribution and/or improved shelf space.

Market research
The process of methodically investigating a potential market for a new product, or of examining the market for an existing product, and the way it has changed (or might be about to change). Market research involves asking a sample of consumers a number of questions about a product, a service or a company. This can be done in many ways: at random on the street, in structured discussion groups, by telephone, or by written questionnaire. The answers can then be analysed statistically in order to examine the (potential) market along a number of different dimensions: age, geography, social status, and so on.

Market share
A company's sales in a particular market expressed as a percentage of total sales in that market. This is a key indicator of a company's competitive position compared with its commercial rivals. Japanese companies lay great store by

market share, often concentrating on it at the expense of PROFIT.

One problem with market share is that it is not always clear what market is being shared. For example, is Mars competing in the market for chocolate bars, for all chocolate, or even for all confectionery? It is no good having 80% of the chocolate-bar market if people have stopped buying bars and are eating boxes of chocolates instead.

MARKET VALUE ADDED

The market VALUE of a company minus the total cash that has been invested in the company. This is the market's measure of how much value has been added by the company and its operations.

MARKETING

According to the Institute of Marketing, this is "the management process of identifying, anticipating and satisfying customer requirements profitably". Another definition is "the process of taking the guesswork out of hunch". Marketing includes functions like ADVERTISING, MARKET RESEARCH, sales PROMOTION and testing new products (TEST MARKETING). In most large companies all these responsibilities come under one marketing department. In smaller businesses, they are either bought in from outside (advertising and market research, in particular), or they are the direct responsibility of someone not far from the chief executive.

Not everything that goes by the name of "marketing" deserves it. It has become too fashionable. A grave-digger remains a grave-digger even when called a mortician. Only the cost of burial goes up.

Peter Drucker

ABRAHAM MASLOW

An influential psychologist who died in 1970. Maslow's most famous theory was that of the hierarchy of needs. He postulated that needs had to be satisfied in sequence. Higher needs could not be tended to until lower ones had been satisfied. Hungry people were unlikely to be creative, for example. In descending order, Maslow's hierarchy was:

- security and self-control;
- social relationships;
- self-esteem;
- status and recognition;
- achievement and challenge;
- power;
- creativity;
- self-actualisation.

This has considerable relevance for the motivation of employees.

MASS PRODUCTION

The production of large quantities of standard items using ECONOMIES OF SCALE to keep the cost of each item as low as possible. In effect, mass production divides labour into the highly skilled, who design sophisticated production systems for the manufacture of goods and services, and the low skilled, who actually operate the systems. It is fundamental to mass production that as much initiative as possible be taken away from the individual worker. This reduces the chance of error and increases the efficiency of the system.

The technology of mass production is inherently violent, ecologically damaging, self-defeating in terms of non-renewable resources, and stultifying for the human person.

E.F. Schumacher

MATRIX MANAGEMENT

A method that was largely devised by a Dutch company, Philips, after the second world war as a means of managing a broad range of products across a broad range of markets. Management controls ran in two directions: horizontally across geographical regions and vertically across different product groups. Individual managers in the field then reported horizontally to the boss of their region and vertically to the boss of their product group. The system was adopted by many other MULTINATIONALS, but it became discredited as Philips itself struggled to make it work in the 1970s and 1980s.

MBA

A postgraduate (and usually post-experience) general training in business and management. In the United States (where most universities now offer degrees in business administration) the Master's Degree in Business Administration (MBA) course usually lasts two years or 21 months; in Europe it is usually condensed into one year; in Japan it does not exist.

Most MBA courses have a core of compulsory subjects plus a number of elective courses from which students can choose those that suit them best. The range of subjects varies, but it usually includes staples such as:

- accounting and finance;
- economics and business policy;
- HUMAN RESOURCE MANAGEMENT;
- MARKETING;
- operations;
- organisational behaviour.

The electives might include such things as international business, INFORMATION TECHNOLOGY, E-COMMERCE and health care management.

It is difficult to be precise about how many MBA programmes are on offer. There are probably some 700 programmes in the United States and perhaps 200 in Europe. These produce well over 100,000 MBA graduates a year, with another 1,000–2,000 graduating from institutions elsewhere. Student intake is as high as 700–900 at leading schools such as Harvard, Kellogg and Wharton in the United States. In the UK and

Europe it is much lower; around 250 at London Business School, for example.

The important thing today is not so much whether a candidate has an MBA, but where he or she got it from. An MBA is no longer of itself a passport to a world of six-figure salaries. The crucial question for aspiring MBA students is which course and institution provide the best value for money. A starting point is the Economist Intelligence Unit's annual *Which MBA?*, a "critical guide to the world's best programmes".

MBO

See MANAGEMENT BUY-OUT.

DOUGLAS MCGREGOR

An American professor at Harvard Business School who, in the early 1960s, came up with one of the most persistently popular management ideas of all time. He classified management styles into two types: THEORY X and THEORY Y, the authoritarian style and the participative style. McGregor died at a comparatively early age, but in the 1990s he was voted the most popular management writer of all time, alongside HENRI FAYOL.

MCKINSEY

A firm of MANAGEMENT CONSULTANTS founded by James McKinsey (1889–1937), an American who was professor of cost accounting at the University of Chicago's Graduate School of Business. He was with the firm for only a few years in the 1920s (until he was offered the job of managing director of Montgomery Ward), but his so-called General Survey – a checklist for effective management consultancy – is still compulsory reading for all new McKinsey recruits.

McKinsey is now the doyen of STRATEGY consultants; the one-time employer of TOM PETERS, Robert Waterman, KENICHI OHMAE and William Hague, leader of the UK's Conservative Party. The MARKET LEADER to whom others aspire, McKinsey was the first to bring American-style management consultancy to the rest of the world. It took Europe by storm when it first arrived there in the 1950s. It was different. It focused on strategy, and its lines of communication were with the top echelons of its clients. Other consultants were left to grub around in the middle ranks.

McKinsey was arguably the biggest single influence on the restructuring of American industry in the 1980s, trail-blazing the fashion for a return to CORE COMPETENCES and eschewing DIVERSIFICATION. It advised, *inter alia*, Citicorp (the world's biggest bank at the time), Merrill Lynch (the world's biggest securities firm at the time) and General Motors (the world's biggest car company at the time).

MEDIA BUYING

The buying of time (in broadcast media) or of space (in published media) for the showing of advertisements. Each ADVERTISING agency used to have its own specialist department for the purpose. However, more and more firms have been setting up as independent media buyers. By pooling the requirements of a number of agencies, they are often able to win bigger discounts from the media.

MENTORING

A method of management training in which junior managers are assigned a specific individual senior manager to whom they have privileged access for advice and guidance. A bit like the tutorial system practised in older universities.

MERGERS AND ACQUISITIONS

The two ways in which companies come together, often abbreviated to M&A. Mergers are friendly combinations of two or more companies into a new entity; acquisitions are the (sometimes unwelcome) TAKEOVER of one company by another. The advantage of the friendliness that exists in mergers can sometimes be counterbalanced by paralysis. BOARDS of DIRECTORS may be simply added together – two Spanish banks that merged ended up with a board of 38 directors. Nobody resigns (because nobody "won") and it is difficult to reap ECONOMIES OF SCALE or to realise promised SYNERGY.

Despite an indifferent track record (fewer than 50% of all mergers and acquisitions are deemed to be a success), managers' enthusiasm for M&A is unabated. So too is the enthusiasm of the lawyers, bankers and consultants who gain significantly from such deals.

I always said that mega-mergers were for megalomaniacs.
David Ogilvy

HENRY MINTZBERG

A Canadian academic who first trained as an engineer, Mintzberg provided some original insight into how organisations work. One of his recurring themes is the superficiality of most managers' work – they rarely spend more than ten minutes on any one issue. In *Mintzberg on Management* he distilled his view of management thus:

> *We end up with a vicious circle in our society. An irrational obsession with rationality produces a society of large, bureaucratic organisations run by a professional management that proves thin, superficial and sometimes immoral. That drives out human commitment, which in turn leads to the politicisation of organisations. This should destroy them, but it does not, for they turn around and use their political power to sustain themselves artificially. Organisations thereby get larger, more bureaucratic, and more politicised, and their managements as a consequence get thinner, more superficial and less moral.*

MISSION STATEMENT

A statement by a company of its overriding business goals, of how it is going to achieve them, and of the values it will uphold in doing so. After a visit to Sears, Roebuck in the United States in the 1920s, the founders of Marks & Spencer, then a rather ordinary general store, redefined their mission as:

> *The subversion of the class structure of nineteenth century England by making available to the working and lower-middle classes, upper-class goods of better than upper-class quality at prices the working and lower-middle classes could well afford.*

Few companies have such a precise (or socially ambitious) mission statement.

Mission statements are seen as a tool for creating team spirit and unity of purpose among a company's workforce, by giving workers an idea of a higher purpose to their labour. To achieve this aim, mission statements must be:

- the result of some sort of consensus throughout the company of what it is about;
- clear and memorable;
- widely known and widely disseminated;
- realistic, and not based on some far-flung ambition that employees cannot relate to.

Modelling

The expounding of mathematical formulae to represent the interrelationships between variables in a company's business or in a country's economy. Once established, these formulae can be fed into a computer program with particular values for a number of chosen variables (in the case of a business these might be price, MARKET SHARE and the cost of materials). The computer model can then almost immediately demonstrate the effect that these values have on other variables.

Modem

A shortened form of modulator-demodulator, the instrument that joins a computer to a telephone line and allows computer-generated messages to be converted into telephonic messages and sent around the world. Without the modem there would be no INTERNET.

MULTINATIONAL
A company that has production and MARKETING operations in more than one country. Multinationals are nothing new. In the early years of the 20th century, American companies such as Kellogg and Singer had a number of production facilities outside the United States. However, these early multinationals operated like a series of independent national operations, largely because communications and transport systems were slow and inefficient. Each national business was forced to plan and operate as an independent unit. Only in recent years (with the help of sophisticated air transport and telecoms) have multinationals been able to think of working as a single unit across the globe.

We used to be an American company with a large international business. Now we're a large international company with a sizeable American business.
Coca-Cola

MULTI-SKILLING
Equipping workers with a number of skills so that they can cover for each other and be more flexible when there is a shortage. Traditionally, each employee had a specific skill for a specific task, which only he or she performed. In today's more flexible working environment, however, employees are expected to carry out a number of different tasks, each requiring different skills. A hotel's wine waiter, for instance, might be expected to work on the reception desk in the mornings, the busiest time for departures and not a time when much wine is called for.

NET PRESENT VALUE
A mathematical formula for measuring the viability of an investment project. Net present value (NPV) is the difference between the present VALUE of the future revenue of the project, and the present value of its future costs. The present value is calculated by discounting the project's future revenues and costs by the cost of its capital.

NETWORK
A term derived from computer language where it refers to the linking of discrete terminals in such a way that each can access data held by the others. Networking also refers to a method used by service firms (such as lawyers and accountants) to build up an international presence without the capital cost of opening offices in lots of cities. Linked together under some sort of umbrella organisation, firms in a number of different countries agree to pool their resources as and when necessary. Loose structures of this sort, however, create problems of their own. Charging for the various little favours that are demanded across the network becomes difficult. Yet depending on strangers to return favours is unreliable. Inevitably, one partner in the network feels unfairly put upon.

Another form of networking is socialising with the aim of gaining some advantage, perhaps a contract for your firm or a job offer for yourself. Meetings of BUSINESS SCHOOL ALUMNI are often good for this sort of networking.

NICHE MARKET
A small, narrowly defined market that can be carefully targeted by a company, particularly one whose products have a limited appeal, such as stamp albums. Niche MARKETING was formerly known as concentrated segmentation.

NON-EXECUTIVE DIRECTOR
A DIRECTOR of a company who does not work in an executive capacity for that company. Good non-executive directors combine general business

knowledge and experience with objectivity, and have the guts to tell a chief executive when they think he is wrong. Many companies have floundered because their non-executive directors have failed to keep a headstrong chief executive in check.

Many companies use HEADHUNTERS to find non-executive directors instead of the more traditional method of trawling among the chairman's friends. More and more of them are seeking to attract foreigners who might be of use in important overseas markets.

Finding good people to fill the role is not easy. Many invitees are concerned about the potential liability of being involved with a company that they do not have day-to-day contact with. Other candidates, who are top-class businessmen elsewhere, have little spare time, and the pay has no attraction for them. One way to ensure commitment is to insist that non-executive directors also be shareholders.

NPV

See NET PRESENT VALUE.

OBJECTIVES

These are the medium-term goals towards which a company strives. At their best they help employees to attain levels of performance that they did not imagine they could be capable of. They also provide yardsticks by which a firm can measure its success.

The best objectives have five qualities. These are:

- precise;
- measurable;
- feasible (that is, achievable);
- consistent; and
- suited to the type of company and industry for which they have been designed.

OEM

See ORIGINAL EQUIPMENT MANUFACTURE.

KENICHI OHMAE

Japan's only world-famous management guru. Ohmae is an un-Japanese individualist who acts as a sophisticated interpreter of corporate Japan to the West. Trained as a nuclear physicist in the United States, he spent most of his career as a MANAGEMENT CONSULTANT with MCKINSEY in Tokyo. Much of his written work, of which there has been a prodigious amount, has been concerned with the new global enterprise: how companies can best spread themselves around the triad of the United States, Europe and East Asia.

People of the same trade seldom meet together, even for merriment and diversion, but the conversation ends in a conspiracy against the public, or in some contrivance to raise prices.

Adam Smith

OLIGOPOLY

The control of an industry by a small number of producers. Oligopolies are found in many industries and they can behave much like monopolies.

They can also be fiercely competitive. Procter & Gamble and Unilever dominate world production of washing powders. Yet every twitch of one makes the other twitch too.

Online

A computer is online if it has direct access to another computer via an open telecommunications link.

Operational research

Called operations research in the United States, but generally referred to everywhere as OR. Operational research is defined by the OR Society as:

> *The application of the methods of science to complex problems arising in the direction and management of large systems of men, machines, materials and money in industry, business, government and defence. The distinctive approach is to develop a scientific model of the system, incorporating measurements of factors, such as chance and risk, with which to predict and compare the outcomes of alternative decisions, strategies or controls. The purpose is to help management determine its policy and action scientifically.*

What more is there to say? Except to add that membership of OR societies has been declining in recent years.

Opportunity cost

The cost of not doing something: a key concept in business economics, but not the sort of cost recognised by accountants. Business always involves making choices, and decision making involves the rejection of opportunities as much as the selection of them. Should a company's resources be allocated to launching an existing product into a new market? Or should they be directed at launching a new product into an existing market? Or maybe the company should just keep its money in the bank. The opportunity cost is the reward that would have come from the best course of action that the business did not follow.

If the choice lies between the production or purchase of two commodities, the value of one is measured by the sacrifice of going without the other.

H.J. Davenport

OPTION

A contract that gives a person the right to buy or sell a commodity, currency or security within a given period of time (usually anything up to nine months) at an agreed price (the striking price). The buyer of the contract pays a small premium for the right to exercise the option.

An option to buy is called a call option, because the holder of the option has the right to call for the commodity (or whatever) from the taker of the option. An option to sell is called a put option, because the holder has the right to put the commodity to the taker at the agreed price.

Options give industry and commerce the chance to fix in advance a price for the raw materials, currency or financial instruments that they will need in the future. There are a growing number of secondary markets where options can be traded between the time that the contract is made and the time that it matures. These give the instruments liquidity.

This type of option should be distinguished from a stock option, which is the right given by companies to selected employees to buy some of the company's shares at a favourable price. Stock options are given as an incentive to attract and retain employees, and they have been a significant factor in luring talented individuals to work for small START-UPS and DOT COMS.

OR

See OPERATIONAL RESEARCH.

Organic growth
The internal growth of an organisation that comes from an expansion of its existing resources. Fast organic growth in terms of sales is often achieved at the expense of profitability. Such growth almost inevitably requires up-front investment in people and plant, and this cuts PROFITS for a while.

Original equipment manufacture
The practice of manufacturing unbranded consumer goods for suppliers who put their name on them and sell them as their own. Original equipment manufacture (OEM) is one manifestation of a battle between retailers and manufacturers for pole position in the hearts and minds of consumers.

Outplacement
Assistance given by an employer to an employee who is being laid off. The service is often provided by specialist outplacement agencies whose main task is to help find the employee a new job or career. The agency may also offer financial advice, counselling to the employee's family, and tips on how to handle job interviews or how to fill in a CV.

Outsource
To hand over to others outside the organisation the responsibility for providing it with materials, components or services. Outsourcing is at least as old as the oldest window cleaner. But it had a renaissance as a result of the corporate fad for focusing on CORE COMPETENCES. Companies began to think about shedding activities that could be carried out more efficiently elsewhere. In particular, they began to outsource their IT requirements, handing over to other firms not only the responsibility for running their IT systems, but also the responsibility for their IT staff. In many cases, the staff moved lock, stock and barrel to the outsourcing organisation.

A company that outsources almost everything becomes a VIRTUAL ORGANISATION, leaving itself free to focus on a very narrow range of activities.

OUTWORKER
A person who carries out part of an industrial PROCESS for a large corporation from their own home or workshop. Outworkers are usually paid at piece rates, that is, according to the quantity of goods they produce. The practice has become popular in a number of modern, high-tech industries. Data processing, for example, is an operation that lends itself well to outworkers.

Despite being trendy, however, outworkers are not new. They existed well before the Industrial Revolution. Early textiles factories in England relied heavily on women putting together garments in their homes. The system is still popular in the textiles industry in developing countries, where work is farmed out to homes and to small independent workshops.

OVERTRADING
The practice of increasing turnover to a level where it is too large to be supported by the other aspects of the business, particularly by its WORKING CAPITAL. The price of too rapid growth, associated mainly with younger businesses. An over-rapid increase in turnover leaves a company vulnerable because it has to finance high levels of INVENTORY (to meet the strong demand) as well as high levels of debt (from its rapid growth in sales). This can leave it short of cash to pay salaries and creditors – in short, in trouble.

Pareto Priniciple

An empirical finding named after Alfredo Pareto, an Italian professor of political economy in Lausanne in the 19th century. The Pareto Principle (often known as the 80/20 rule) states that a large proportion of the activity in a market is always accounted for by a small number of operators; for example, 80% of a company's PROFIT comes from 20% of its products.

Pareto himself found this to be true of the income distribution of countries, and discovered (incidentally) that distributions are generally the same whatever the country. Extending this brought him to Pareto's Law: that the only way to increase the income of the poorest members of society is by increasing production overall, that is, GDP. In other words, redistribution does not work.

Parkinson's Law

The title of a book, first published in 1958 and written by a history professor called Cyril Northcote Parkinson. The book was one of the first about management to be written in a humorous style, and it made a satirical stab at the self-satisfied behaviour of managers within large organisations. It had a wide influence and was translated into many languages.

The book contained a number of "laws", of which the most famous is probably: "Work expands to fill the time available for its completion." Allied to this is the principle that: "Expenditure rises to meet income." Others include an observation about management meetings: "The less important the subject; the more animated the discussion."

Partnership

An association of people formed to do business and make a PROFIT without being incorporated as a company. In general, partnerships do not enjoy the comfort of LIMITED LIABILITY. Partners are individually responsible for the debts of the partnership.

There is, however, something called a limited

partnership. In this there are two types of partner: limited partners and general partners. Limited partners take no financial responsibility beyond the capital that they originally contribute to the business. General partners are like partners in any normal partnership.

Limited partnerships have been particularly popular and successful in Germany. They neatly get around the problem that unlimited partnerships often have in raising capital for expansion.

PATENT

The right granted to inventors to have a monopoly on the MARKETING of their inventions for a certain specified period of time. The right is registered at a patent office, which first does a search to determine whether the invention is new. While such a search is taking place, inventors can sell their products with the postscript: "Patent Pending".

Obtaining patents around the world is such a complicated business that there are professional patent AGENTS to help inventors protect their property. Some inventors (like big drugs companies) complain that patents (usually given for 15–20 years) do not last long enough. By the time the companies have got all the official approvals needed for a drug to be put on sale, much of the life of the patent has expired.

To extend the life, some inventors take out different patents on different aspects of their invention. Each one is designed to expire on a different date, and also designed to frustrate and confuse potential copycats.

PAYBACK PERIOD

The time it takes for an ASSET or investment to pay for itself. For a new machine, the payback period is the time that it takes to save (or earn) as much as the machine cost. The payback comes through more efficient and less costly production, or through greater PRODUCTIVITY. For an investment, the payback period is the time that it takes for the returns to equal the investment.

P/E RATIO

The ratio of a company's stockmarket price (P) to its earnings (E), the price/earnings ratio. This ratio is a closely watched figure among stockbrokers and investment bankers. It provides a means of comparing the performance of very different corporate entities, and it gives some indication of whether a company's shares are undervalued or overvalued.

The P/E ratio compares a company's stockmarket VALUE (that is, its number of shares multiplied by its share price) with its latest annual after-tax profits. Put it the other way round, and the ratio is a measure of how many years it would take investors to get their money back if the company were to keep its PROFITS constant and to distribute all of them every year.

PERFORMANCE-RELATED PAY

There are a number of schemes that relate an employee's remuneration to his or her performance. In such schemes, managers are guaranteed a comparatively small salary and the rest of their pay depends on profits or sales or a similar indicator. In 1989 ICI introduced performance-related pay for all its 25,000 white-collar workers. It threw out a system of job evaluation that had been the basis of its salary structure for 20 years, stating that it needed to give greater recognition of "individual performance and contribution to the company". This involved decentralising much of the assessment and training of staff to local managers.

The key to such schemes lies in the pre-agreed criteria for the assessment of performance. Several schemes for senior managers have been criticised because the criteria were set by the same people who benefited from them.

PETER PRINICIPLE

The principle that every man or woman eventually rises to his or her level of incompetence. First enunciated by Laurence J. Peter in a book published in 1969, the principle (also known as "cream rises until it sours") has become deeply embedded in management myth. Managers are presumed to be promoted whenever they do jobs competently. They stop being promoted when their "final PROMOTION" takes them to a job that they do incompetently.

Thus Peter's corollary says that "in time, every post tends to be occupied by an employee who is incompetent to carry out its duties". Companies are only kept alive because work is being done by those who have yet to reach their level of incompetence.

Peter revelled in the ailments of those who had got their final promotion. They included the following, which seem as applicable to today's IT age as they were in the paper-based 1960s.

- Galloping phonophilia. The use of two or more phones to keep in touch with subordinates (mobile ones today).
- Papyrophobia. Obsessive clearing of the desk.
- Fileophilia. The frequent opening of new files (electronic ones today).

Peter recommended that managers demonstrate "creative incompetence" in order to avoid making that final promotion. One way is to park occasionally in the space reserved exclusively for the company chairman.

A variation on the Peter Principle, called the Paula Principle, says that women always stay below their level of incompetence, because they hold themselves back from promotion.

TOM PETERS

The author of *In Search of Excellence* (with Robert Waterman) and *Thriving on Chaos*. When he started writing books, Peters was a MANAGEMENT CONSULTANT with MCKINSEY, and much of the case material that gives the books their special appeal was culled from his experience as a consultant. Since his success he has lectured all over the world. He is as ebullient as a speaker as he is as a writer.

In Search of Excellence was a phenomenon, selling over 5m copies around the world. "I think we did a service to industry by reintroducing customers into the language," said Peters of Waterman and himself. At the book's core was the simple idea that the chief concerns of excellent companies are the care of customers, innovation and people. It was a eulogy to instinct.

In the late 1980s Peters again popularised a leading undercurrent in management thinking: the need to live with constant change.

Piece rate
A method of rewarding workers based on the number of units that they produce. It differs from the more common way of paying employees according to the number of hours that they work. On some occasions the two methods of rewarding labour are combined. Workers receive a minimum wage that is topped up by a commission relating to the amount of goods (above a minimum) that they sell or produce.

Platform
Originally used of computers to refer to the combination of an operating system (software) and a processor (hardware) on top of which other programs can be run. But the word has now gained wider coinage in business and refers to any combination of resources on which a VALUE-adding business or operation can be built.

PMM
See POST-MERGER MANAGEMENT.

Portal
A site on the WORLD WIDE WEB that selects other sites which it suggests to visitors (to its site) might be of interest. AOL, Lycos, MSN, Netscape and Yahoo are well-known examples of portals.

Michael Porter
One of the youngest professors ever at Harvard Business School. Porter's work is concerned with

giving companies a framework in which to think about how they can compete more successfully. A quote illustrates his method:

> *A systematic way of examining all the activities a firm performs and how they interact is essential for analysing the sources of competitive advantage ... the value chain disaggregates a firm into its strategically relevant activities in order to understand the behaviour of costs and the existing and potential sources of differentiation.*

Porter is one of the most sought-after speakers on the lucrative management lecture circuit (along with TOM PETERS). Like Peters he takes the quite complicated theoretical concepts of others (economic concepts) and packages them in an easily digestible form for busy managers.

Porter's analysis of a company's competitive position is based on what have become notorious as the "Five Forces":

- The existing rivalry between firms in the business.
- The threat of new entrants coming into the market.
- The threat of substitute products or services.
- The bargaining power of suppliers.
- The bargaining power of buyers.

PORTFOLIO MANAGEMENT

The study of how best to MANAGE a diversified range of businesses under one corporate umbrella. One of the most influential ideas in the area has been the GROWTH SHARE MATRIX, devised by the BOSTON CONSULTING GROUP as a means to determine how to allocate cash among competing claimants within the same organisation. The dominant idea now is that of CORE COMPETENCES, that companies should identify what it is that they do best and then assemble their portfolio of businesses around those competences (or skills).

Portfolio theory
The theory that it is better (in the sense that it is less risky) to invest in a portfolio of ASSETS over the long term than it is to put all your eggs in one basket. When a pension fund starts to buy Impressionist paintings or a paper company starts buying software firms, they are both attempting to reduce their risks (and thereby to improve their returns) by diversifying into a portfolio of investments.

Positioning
The attempt to give a product or service a specific identity by emphasising its distinctive features. This helps consumers to know what they're getting when they choose that particular product. One washing-up liquid, for example, might position itself as being especially kind to the hands of the washer-up. Another might emphasise the fact that it is low-priced and reliable. Each would be taking up a slightly different position in the market, hoping thereby to optimise its returns.

Post-merger management
It is reckoned that more than half of all MERGERS AND ACQUISITIONS fail to achieve their goals. Many are believed to fail not because the goals themselves are unattainable, but because the management of the new entity in the immediate aftermath of the merger is inadequate. This has put a spotlight on what is known as post-merger management (PMM), those management practices that are relevant to the unique circumstances immediately following a merger. Most commentators place the greatest emphasis during PMM on merging the different organisations' cultures. Several cross-border mergers in recent years have been notorious for the refusal of the different companies' managers to work together.

PPP
See PURCHASING POWER PARITY.

PR
See PUBLIC RELATIONS.

PREDATORY PRICING
The practice of dramatically cutting prices with the specific aim of stealing MARKET SHARE from existing competitors. The problem with predatory pricing is what to do when the market share has been stolen. If you return prices to their original level then you become vulnerable to somebody else's predatory pricing. But if you retain them at their new low level there might not be much (if any) PROFIT in it for you.

PREFERRED SUPPLIER
Large manufacturing companies used to use hundreds of different suppliers, switching between them regularly in a continuous attempt to find the cheapest source of materials. In recent years, however, a number of companies have realised that in the longer term this may not be the best (or the cheapest) way to do things. They have chosen to limit their suppliers to a short list of what are called preferred suppliers. Such suppliers are determined centrally, but different parts of the corporation are not compelled to use them. However, the firm's internal systems are designed to encourage them to do so.

PRIVATISATION
The process of selling off state-owned businesses to the private sector. Privatisation is usually seen as a way of injecting competition and entrepreneurship into fossilised state-owned monopolies. But whatever it is, it is certainly not an overnight cure. A utility employing hundreds of thousands of people does not become dashing and dynamic overnight just because a few pieces of paper change hands. The management's frame of mind has to change too, and that can take some time.

PROCESS
A group of activities in a business which, when

put together, create VALUE for a customer. The fundamental unit of the ADDED VALUE approach to business. In this framework, superior business performance becomes a matter of striving for ever better processes, that is, for process excellence.

A process may be just one small part of manufacturing, or it may be the whole of a big operation such as MARKETING (the marketing process). Dividing organisations into a series of such processes, linked together in a VALUE CHAIN, is a popular way of viewing corporate structure. The process is at the heart of BUSINESS PROCESS RE-ENGINEERING.

PROCESS ARCHITECTURE

The design of a PROCESS. The ordering and carrying out of the activities that make up a process in such a way that they improve the overall performance of the organisation.

PRODUCT DEVELOPMENT

The systematic evolution of a product to ensure that it is not stranded by changing consumer tastes. Some products (like Kellogg's cornflakes or Bovril) have been selling successfully for decades without seeming to change at all. Yet their packaging has changed subtly, and so has the image presented by their ADVERTISING. (So too has their taste, but nobody has a record of what that used to be like.)

One popular view of product development is that products go through a biological-style life cycle. They are born; they are introduced into the market (in a sort of product version of the debutante's ball); they grow (in terms of their sales); they mature (their sales growth stops); and then they decline into old age (as their sales fall off).

Many products, however, seem to get stuck somewhere in mid-life. A remarkable number of market-leading products in the United States are the same today as they were 60 years ago.

PRODUCTIVITY

Literally, the output produced by a unit of one of

the three FACTORS OF PRODUCTION within a given period of time. Thus there is the productivity of labour (the output per employee), the productivity of land and the productivity of capital. For the most part, increasing productivity is a gradual process. But occasionally there are inventions that enable it to make a quantum leap. For example, the computer makes a one-off improvement in the productivity of all of us; a new motorway sharply improves that of lorry drivers; a new financial market (like the commercial paper market in the United States) can boost that of capital; and a new fertiliser or strain of seed is able to improve dramatically the productivity of land.

PROFIT

To accountants, profit is the excess of a company's revenue over its costs. It is the ultimate figure in the PROFIT AND LOSS ACCOUNT. If a company's costs exceed its revenue during a period then it has made a loss.

To economists, profit is the reward to ENTREPRENEURS for taking the risks of doing business. It is what is left from the price of goods when rewards have been paid to the FACTORS OF PRODUCTION, such as salaries to labour, rent for land and interest (or dividends) on capital.

The accountants' idea of profit is far from being precise. Whenever two accountants look at one company's books they find at least three profits.

There are many different ways of using the word:

- After-tax profit. The gross profit less tax.
- Attributable profit. Profit that can be attributed to a particular division or department of an organisation.
- Gross profit. The profit before the deduction of things like tax and exceptional payments.
- Monopoly profit. The exceptional profit that a firm can earn if it has a monopoly in a particular market.
- Net profit. The gross profit less tax and other exceptional payments.

- Paper profit. A profit that has been earned but not yet realised, like that from a rise in the share price of a company whose shares an investor has not yet sold.
- Retained profit. The profit that is left to a company after absolutely everything else has been paid (including dividends).
- Windfall profit. An unexpected profit that suddenly appears from nowhere (through a currency devaluation, perhaps, or after the death of Uncle Tom).

PROFIT AND LOSS ACCOUNT

The profit and loss account, commonly known as the P&L account and referred to in the United States as the income statement, is one of the two main financial statements to appear in a company's annual report. (The other is the BALANCE SHEET.)

The balance sheet takes a snapshot of a company's financial condition on the last day of its financial year, and the P&L account is a record of its revenue and expenditure during that year. Managers produce more frequent P&L statements for their own internal purposes (or to meet the demands of stockmarkets). But the legal requirement is usually for an audited statement to be produced for each distinct company once a year.

P&L accounts differ from country to country in the amount of detail that they show. Most of the differences lie in the footnotes, which have increasingly begun to dwarf the accounts themselves.

PROFIT CENTRE

A discrete unit within an organisation that is responsible for its own PROFIT; in other words, a unit that can produce its own self-contained PROFIT AND LOSS ACCOUNT. In theory, such centres encourage managers to be entrepreneurial and more financially responsible. In practice, no unit is an island, and there are always certain decisions affecting the bottom line of a profit centre that are outside its managers' control (decisions on inter-group pricing, for example). This can create internal resentment and outweigh some of the advantages that come from divesting responsibility.

Profit sharing

An arrangement between the employees and the owners of a business whereby the employees receive an agreed amount of the company's PROFIT to be shared among themselves. In practice, profit-sharing schemes often fall foul of internal jealousies. One of the most common is between departments that know they made the biggest contribution to profits and departments that do not believe the figures.

The idea of making workers share in profits is a very attractive one and it would seem that it is from there that harmony between capital and labour should come. But the practical formula for such sharing has not yet been found.

Henri Fayol

Project finance

The financing of a specific project where the financier relies on the project (and the project alone) for security and for a return. It is a technique particularly suited to the financing of large public-sector projects in impoverished developing countries, such as a dam in Pakistan or a motorway in Malaysia. The (Western) banks that lend the money for such projects secure the loans on the dam or motorway and rely on the stream of income from the electricity that the dam produces or from the tolls that the road collects for their repayment.

Promotion

A special one-off effort to increase the sales of a product or service. This may be done through an ADVERTISING campaign specially designed for the purpose, or by means of special displays at trade shows or retail outlets.

Promotion can also, of course, refer to the

elevation of an individual employee to a more senior status within their organisation.

Protectionism

The art of preventing potential commercial rivals from entering a market or a country. Governments indulge in protectionism by writing laws that protect their home industries from foreign competition. By and large, industries encourage them in this, and they do what they can to erect their own BARRIERS TO ENTRY that effectively protect their markets.

Industrialists who claim that they are not protectionists at heart are probably lying. There is no easier business life than being a manufacturer who is sheltered behind high tariff walls while supplying an unsophisticated market with basic goods. All governments that profess to pursue free trade policies find themselves at times in conflict with those who are supposed to be the biggest beneficiaries from such policies: their own country's business community.

Public relations

The relations between a corporation and its public, and the management of those relations. A company's public consists of a wide range of constituents: investors, customers, employees, legislators, environmentalists, and so on. The traditional way to reach these external audiences is through the media (the press, television and radio), via press releases and press conferences, and by arranging interviews with key people in the organisation.

Some companies employ outside public relations (PR) consultants; others employ full-time specialists in-house. The largest companies often use a combination of both. (See also INVESTOR RELATIONS.)

Pump priming

An extra bit of effort and energy is required to get a pump flowing at the beginning, after which it carries on with little effort. This phenomenon has an obvious analogy in business. Whether it is for an entirely new business or for a new development in a large old business, pump priming is essential. Finding finance for pump priming, however, is notoriously difficult, partly because it is needed at what is just about the most risky time in a product or business's life.

PURCHASING POWER PARITY

A method of comparing living standards among countries that does not rely on simplistically dividing GDP per head figures by current market exchange rates. The purchasing power parity (PPP) method takes a basket of goods and services and finds out how much it costs in each country's currency. Comparing those costs gives a real exchange rate in terms of the purchasing power of different currencies.

Using simple exchange rates to compare incomes among countries is misleading for two reasons. First, exchange rates are influenced only by goods and services that are traded internationally (and so exclude things like housing). Second, exchange rates can swing wildly from one year to another because of volatile capital flows. So when comparing living standards in different countries, the United States comes about ninth in the world using GDP per head as the measure but second in PPP terms.

PYRAMID SELLING

A system of selling products by setting up a pyramid of AGENTS. The first agent sells a quantity of the products to other agents (for a commission), and each of them then sells products to a number of others (again for a commission), and so (in theory) *ad infinitum*. Except that agents soon start treading on each other's toes as their potential markets increasingly overlap. Because it has had a particular fascination for fraudsters, pyramid selling has been made illegal in some countries.

QUALITY CIRCLE

A system devised by the Japanese whereby shop-floor workers are grouped into teams. Each team is responsible for undertaking certain tasks, and for the quality of those tasks. The leader of a team is called the circle facilitator.

The method relies heavily on charts recording quantitative measures of performance over time. The top performers are rewarded with praise and perks. In the early 1980s quality circles were seen as the panacea for all the labour-relations ailments of the Western world.

To their surprise, however, many Western companies faced fierce resistance to quality circles from their employees. This was often because they were being imposed willy-nilly on existing organisational structures. Quality circles then gave way in popularity to TOTAL QUALITY MANAGEMENT, an American-inspired method that attempts to integrate quality into existing management structures.

QUALITY CONTROL

Testing a sample of products before they are shipped to a buyer to see if they are of the specified quality. A certain tolerance of error may be acceptable in the sample (say, 5%). Anything above that and buyers will demand further checks. If the faults are large and extensive they can refuse to take the goods.

It is difficult for companies that are importing goods from far away to carry out rigorous quality-control checks, but there are firms (agencies) that specialise in carrying out checks on their behalf.

Managers have come to realise that it is pointless to learn at the end of the production PROCESS, just before the customer is about to take delivery, that their goods are no good. It is much better for quality control to begin when the first step in the production process is taken. Hence the emphasis on TOTAL QUALITY MANAGEMENT.

Rate of return

The reward from an investment expressed as a percentage of the original sum invested. The reward includes both capital gain and income. This provides a crude way of comparing the relative attractions of a number of different investments. Is it more rewarding to place $10,000 today in an interest-earning bank account and leave it there for five years, or to give it to your nephew for his new Guatemalan fast-food business, which he hopes to turn into an IPO within five years?

The rate of return is a crude method of comparison because it takes no account of time. Most of the reward from the fast-food business will come as capital gain in five years. The reward from the bank is the interest paid at regular intervals throughout the five years. (See DISCOUNTED CASHFLOW and NET PRESENT VALUE.)

Note also that the rate of return takes no account of differing degrees of certainty. The bank interest is almost as safe as houses; the nephew's prospective capital gain is not.

There are a number of measures of a company's rate of return.

- Return on sales. A simple measure of the percentage of each item sold that is retained as PROFIT; sometimes known as the margin.
- Return on ASSETS. The amount earned by an organisation during a particular period of time expressed as a percentage of the organisation's average total assets during the period. This measures the profitability of the assets employed in the business.
- Return on equity. The basic return to ordinary shareholders; that is, the profit after interest, taxes and preference shareholders' dividends expressed as a percentage of the equity employed.
- Return on investment. The amount earned on a particular investment (in stocks and shares, or in bricks and mortar) expressed as a percentage of the total cost of the investment.

RECIPROCITY
A sort of tit-for-tat in international trade. "You let my x into your country and I'll let your y into mine"; or, obversely, "You stop letting my x into your country and I'll stop letting your y into mine". Reciprocity deals are struck between pairs of countries or between pairs of trading blocs. They are extremely unpopular with the guardians of the world's free trading system.

RE-ENGINEERING
See BUSINESS PROCESS RE-ENGINEERING.

R&D
Short for research and development, that part of industry where scientists and designers search for new products and for new ways of developing existing products. Research refers to the work of pure scientists, such as chemists and engineers. Development is more concerned with creating marketable products out of the findings of the researchers. It is sometimes assumed that this is an inferior skill, but great breakthroughs in research are rare. The company that continually develops its products is more assured of a long and successful future.

Expenditure on research rarely brings quick returns. In some fields it can take 10–20 years from the dawning of an idea to its full commercial exploitation. This is at least twice as long as the average life span of a chief executive.

Some industries are more dependent on R&D than others. The pharmaceuticals industry's success, for instance, is closely related to the ability of white-coated scientists to come up with new drugs in their laboratories.

REGRESSION ANALYSIS
A statistical technique for finding the best fit for a series of plots made on a chart. It has many applications in business. Consider, for example, a number of readings of sales figures for a certain product at a number of different prices. These readings may seem to be randomly spread about

a general tendency for higher prices to mean lower sales. Regression analysis gives the line that is the closest fit to all the readings. Extrapolating this line then gives the best guess for what the product's sales will be at any particular price level.

What regression analysis cannot take into account is the influence of other factors on the readings. For example, how each one might have been influenced by the amount of ADVERTISING going on at the time, or by a change in the product's retail outlets. Some statistics enthusiasts attempt to make three-dimensional figures out of several different regression analyses, each using different variables.

Resources

All the items that are of use to an organisation. These include the tangible and INTANGIBLE ASSETS that appear on a company's BALANCE SHEET. They also include many items that do not appear on a balance sheet; for example, loyal customers, or prime shelf space in the supermarket.

The concept of resources is at the heart of a currently popular view of the corporation as a dynamic system – a set of resources that act and interact with each other in a continuous and dynamic way.

I have come to the conclusion that the decisive change which underlies the rise of organisations is the shift from viewing the worker as a cost centre to viewing him as a resource.

Peter Drucker

Restraint of trade

The part of a contract that imposes a restriction on one of the parties to the contract. Such restrictions usually take one of two forms.

- A restriction on a buyer's ability to purchase goods elsewhere. For instance, for decades most of the UK's pubs were tied to buying beer from only one manufacturer. A free

house was a pub that was free to buy its beer from several suppliers. It usually advertised the fact on its sign outside.
- A restriction on an employee's capacity to work subsequently for a competitor.

In many countries, contracts that contain a restraint of trade are legally invalid, unless the contract is between parties of roughly equal bargaining power who are in a position to look after themselves, or if there is good reason for the restraint – for example, if an employer is merely protecting its legal right to its trade secrets or PATENTS.

RETURN ON ASSETS
See RATE OF RETURN.

RETURN ON EQUITY
See RATE OF RETURN.

RETURN ON INVESTMENT
See RATE OF RETURN.

RETURN ON SALES
See RATE OF RETURN.

RISK ANALYSIS
Assessing the chances of doing a particular piece of business and of not being paid for it. Risk analysis is particularly important when a company is starting to do business with a new customer and is providing that customer with credit facilities. When the customer is in a foreign country there are extra dimensions to the risk, arising from the chance that the customer's currency will be devalued, or that the customer will be nationalised and the state renege on its debts.

Satisficing

A concept that undermines the classical economists' view that human behaviour is determined by a search for what is best among a number of alternatives. Satisficing is the choosing of an option (not necessarily the best) that reaches a minimum acceptable level. It recognises that in many instances where they have to make decisions, human beings are unable to consider all the options available. They therefore go for the one that best meets their minimum standards. They are satisficers, not maximisers.

Managers are also often satisficers, opting for targets and achievements that are acceptable to their firm and to their industry. If they make a determined attempt to maximise their performance they may find that they can soar way above the industry norms.

SBU

See STRATEGIC BUSINESS UNIT.

Scenario planning

Everything in the future is uncertain. But for the purposes of living with the present, certain macroeconomic, social and scientific assumptions have to be made. The classic way of doing this is to extrapolate from the past and to assume that the future will be a continuation of that past.

If this were ever true, it is less so now. Dissatisfaction with extrapolation has led to the development of an alternative way of thinking about the future. Called scenario planning, it involves gathering a group of people together and encouraging them to imagine (given their particular knowledge and expertise) how the future might be. It is not an entirely unstructured process. Ideally, it makes use of a moderator who steers the group towards useful conclusions, for instance, by identifying what might constitute an early warning signal of some dramatic change about to take place in their industry.

Scenario planning was been credited with helping the Pentagon to think about the end of the cold war long before it came about, and of helping Royal Dutch/Shell to cope well with the sharp swings in the price of petrol brought about by OPEC in the 1970s.

Scenarios are stories about the way the world might turn out tomorrow, stories that can help us recognise and adapt to changing aspects of our present environment. They form a method for articulating the different pathways that might exist for you tomorrow, and finding your appropriate movements down each of those possible paths.

Peter Schwartz, *The Art of the Long View*

FRITZ SCHUMACHER

An unconventional German-born economist who spent much of his life working for the UK's National Coal Board. He published an influential collection of essays in 1973, which ensured that his reputation would live long after him. The book also brought a new phrase to the English language. It was entitled *Small is Beautiful.*

The essays were heavily influenced by the time that Schumacher spent advising the Burmese government in the late 1960s. Among other things, he advocated the use of intermediate technology by developing countries instead of a sudden leap into heavy industry. At the time, these countries believed they had no option but to follow the belching-chimney, ASSEMBLY LINE model of industrialisation pioneered in Europe and the United States.

Schumacher's ideas suited their time. In the early 1970s the corporatist state, concentrated on huge private and state-owned companies, seemed to be grinding to a halt. It was ready for a reminder that small could be beautiful.

SEARCH ENGINE

A type of software that enables people to search for things on electronic databases, particularly on the WORLD WIDE WEB. However, the ability of search engines to comb the increasing vastness of the web is more and more limited. Few of them cover as many as a quarter of the sites in existence, and most of them offer a selection that is too unintelligent to be of real use to users.

Securitisation

The switch from corporate reliance on bank loans for finance to securities, such as bonds, equities and commercial paper. In most developed countries there was a sharp shift away from bank finance to securities in the later years of the 20th century.

Seed money

The first small investment in a project. Unlikely to be enough to get the project fully off the ground, seed money should nevertheless be enough to finance, say, a bit of MARKET RESEARCH that will convince a bank to back the project more fully.

Segmentation

The categorising of consumers into a number of different segments, each of which has a distinctive feature. The categorising may be done according to basic demographic features, such as age, sex, country of residence, and so on. Or it may be done according to less precise lifestyle criteria, such as Generation Xers, baby-boomers or empty-nesters.

The purpose of segmentation is to identify more precisely the target market for a particular product or service. Surprisingly few products can genuinely hope to appeal to everybody. Even something like beer is consumed largely by a comparatively small number of young males with a distinctive lifestyle.

Peter Senge

The author of an influential book, *The Fifth Discipline*, published in 1990, which promoted the idea of using computer models to aid business decision making. Senge's fifth discipline is systems thinking. The rapid growth of the power and extent of INFORMATION TECHNOLOGY has allowed managers at all levels of an organisation to use computer models, if only they know how.

You can only understand the system of a rainstorm by contemplating the whole, not any individual part of the pattern … business and other human endeavours are also systems … systems thinking [makes] the full patterns clearer and helps us see how to change them effectively.

Peter Senge

SENSITIVITY ANALYSIS

The study of how sensitive a set of assumptions is to variations. Applied to a BUSINESS PLAN, sensitivity analysis consists of asking a series of "what if" questions. In the plan there will be a number of assumptions about such things as future sales, wages, transport costs, and so on. What happens if sales are, say, 10% less than has been assumed for the year after next? And what if wages increase by 15% instead of the assumed 10% for that year?

From the answers to these questions can be built a matrix of possible outcomes for the business. This will show how sensitive the plan is to different variables, and what is the worst-case scenario. This could be so horrendous that the plan is abandoned altogether, even though it might look potentially profitable should things go reasonably well.

SEVEN Ss

Seven qualities (each of them beginning with the letter S) that were identified in a best-selling book (*The Art of Japanese Management*) as being the areas in which Japanese companies excelled over American companies. The book was written by Richard Pascale and came out a year before the even better-selling *In Search of Excellence* by TOM PETERS and Robert Waterman. Pascale, Peters and Waterman all worked together at the management consultants MCKINSEY, where they gleaned much of the basic research for their respective books.

The Seven Ss have become a well-established framework for thinking about management tasks. They are STRATEGY, STRUCTURE, systems, style, shared values, skills and staff. The first three were called the hard Ss and the last four the soft Ss. Pascale believed that Japanese companies made the hard Ss more productive by allying them better with the soft Ss than did Western companies.

SHRINKAGE
The stock that disappears from a business without ever being recorded in the cash register. Shrinkage consists mostly of goods that are damaged, stolen or (in the case of perishables) thrown away or given away.

SIMULATION
A computer program that represents real situations mathematically. In a simulator a pilot learns how to land a plane without actually having to land a plane. Simulations are used in business to create business games in which teams feed data into computers about markets, prices, and so on, to try out strategic options in comparative safety. Needless to say, there is no way to simulate a pig-headed AGENT or similarly strange behaviour.

ALFRED SLOAN
The man described by Lee Iacocca as "the greatest genius ever in the auto business". Alfred Sloan also wrote one of the first great business biographies, *My Years with General Motors*, and was honoured by his alma mater, the Massachusetts Institute of Technology (MIT), which named a business school after him.

Between 1923, when he became president of a rather rickety General Motors, and the end of the second world war, Sloan transformed the company into the largest and most profitable car manufacturer in the world. He did it by finding a special balance between central authority and DECENTRALISATION. He was personally involved in the selection of every single GM executive, but he gave those executives considerable power to run their own operations.

One notably contrary view of Sloan and his book comes from James O'Toole, an American management professor, who points out: "For the first 300 pages or so, Sloan seems oblivious to the fact that there are any employees in the company ... by reading this book [my students] learn which management practices to avoid."

SME

Short for small and medium-sized enterprises, the lifeblood of a country's industry. Small firms account for a disproportionately high percentage of both companies and INNOVATION everywhere, a fact recognised by most governments through the special tax rates and special agencies (such as the Small Business Administration in the United States) set up to provide soft loans and other support services for them.

Few, if any, firms are born big. They start small, and some grow. Many governments believe that small firms, especially when they are in significant high-tech industries, need protection, particularly from foreign competition, until they reach a sustainable size.

E.F. SCHUMACHER, the author of *Small is Beautiful*, maintained that small was so beautiful that "organisations should imitate nature, which does not allow a single cell to become too large".

Small firms have smaller firms upon their backs to bite 'em. And smaller firms have smaller firms, and so ad infinitum.

Harold Wilson, a former British prime minister, in the Wilson Committee report on the British financial system

---

SOLE TRADER

Businesses (like small shopkeepers) that trade only on their own account. They may have employees, but whatever PROFIT they make is destined for their own pockets.

Sourcing
The continuous process of finding (and then using) sources of goods and raw materials.

Spam
Unsolicited E-MAIL, a growing problem for people who do not want their mail boxes to be overflowing with electronic offers, an unpleasant proportion of which are likely to be pornographic. Spam is growing even more rapidly than unsolicited mail through the traditional postal services, partly because it is virtually costless to the spammer, the person who sends it.

Span of control
The number of people that any one manager can cope with under his or her direct control. There are many different theories about what is the ideal number. It certainly varies from individual to individual, and it certainly has a significant bearing on the structure of organisations. The most popular number for the ideal span of control is around seven.

Spreadsheet
A type of computer program that is particularly useful in areas of business such as planning, BUDGETING and investment appraisal. It enables the user to change one variable in a string of complicated mathematical relationships, and then allows the computer to roll out the effect on all the other variables.

Stakeholders
The wide range of constituencies that have a stake in a corporation's activities. These constituencies range from suppliers to employees to customers to governments. They also include shareholders. At different times in business history, and in different industrial societies, certain stakeholders have gained power and influence at the expense of others. In the UK and the United States, the shareholder has been king for some time. But the customer is making a comeback.

STANDARDISATION
The process of getting rid of variety. This can apply to a production line on which it is more efficient to produce only two standardised products rather than 13 or 30. Or it can apply to an industry or a group of countries like the members of the European Union, which agree to certain standards that their products must meet. Such standards may be applied to the dimensions or contents of the products, and may be produced for perfectly sound reasons like safety. They may also be produced for perfectly unsound reasons, like the need to find work for idle bureaucrats.

START-UP
A business that is just beginning. The start-up cost is the money that such a business needs before it begins to trade. Those involved in start-ups have four main places to look for money:

- their own pockets, or those of family and friends;
- commercial banks;
- special government funds;
- VENTURE CAPITAL.

Governments are keen to see a healthy crop of start-ups in order to rejuvenate their country's corporate stock, which is constantly being depleted by bankruptcies. But raising start-ups is like raising children: give them too much support and they collapse as soon as the support is removed; give them too little and they collapse before it can ever be removed.

Every entrepreneur is a kind of outsider ... the outsiders of one generation become the insiders of the next.

Anthony Sampson

STRATEGIC BUSINESS UNIT
The smallest unit within a corporation that can independently put a STRATEGY into effect. A strategic

business unit (SBU), sometimes known as a strategy centre, can (in theory) be divested and run as a stand-alone business.

STRATEGIC INTENT

A concept first put forward by two business professors, Gary Hamel and C.K. Prahalad, in a *Harvard Business Review* article of the same name. Strategic intent is the broad long-term objective of a corporation, and it is often encapsulated in those snappy phrases beloved by the Japanese, such as Komatsu's "Encircle Caterpillar". Such intent can act as a beacon for everybody in an organisation for many years.

Corporate strategy is the pattern of decisions in a company that determines and reveals its objectives, purposes or goals, produces the principal policies and plans for achieving those goals, and defines the range of business the company is to pursue.

Kenneth R. Andrews, *The Concept of Corporate Strategy*

STRATEGY

The way in which a corporation decides to go about achieving its future goals, and the setting of those goals. Strategy work is usually considered to be the most cerebral part of management activity, suitable only for those at the top of the management ladder. Among MANAGEMENT CONSULTANTS, strategy consulting is considered to be the *crème de la crème.*

Strategy has been subject to a number of fashions over the years. In its early days, it was heavily influenced by military strategy, as many senior managers had spent their early careers in the armed forces. The talk then was of "attacking markets" and "defeating rivals". Then strategy became more focused on matching a business's future resources to its future opportunities. This was the era of long-term planning, when huge planning departments cluttered up corporate headquarters.

Disillusionment with this sort of strategy led to a dramatic slimming down of the concept, to such an extent that strategy eventually became little more than the creation of a rallying cry (or MISSION STATEMENT), around which a corporation could focus its efforts in a non-specific way.

STRUCTURE

The way in which an organisation is organised – one of the SEVEN SS. A business historian, ALFRED CHANDLER, called his first great book *Strategy and Structure*, and suggested that all successful companies must have a structure that is determined by their STRATEGY, and that therefore fits that strategy. As strategy changes, so must structure. Chandler found, however, that in situations where there was little or no competition, structure did not change to match changing strategy. It only did so if it made a difference competitively.

In designing a business's structure, managers must pay attention to:

- the allocation of specific tasks to individuals;
- the grouping of individuals doing similar tasks into specialist departments, such as production and distribution;
- the setting up of systems to facilitate communication and co-ordination between departments;
- the allocation of responsibilities within each department;
- the distribution of authority throughout the organisation.

SUBSTITUTION

The use of one product that is a close substitute for another, for example, margarine for butter. The term is used with particular reference to consumer behaviour when the price of a product rises. What will be the substitution of butter for every 10 cent rise in the price of margarine? Not all possible substitutions for a manufacturer's products will be immediately obvious to it as it considers a price rise.

Succession planning
The task that many people argue is the most important for a chief executive: choosing his or her successor. Mortimer Feinberg, an American expert on the subject, lays down certain guidelines for those who have to make such choices.

- Choose early, disclose late.
- Draw the invisible organisation chart; that is, the differences between titular equals.
- Identify the hidden influential people in the company.
- Spell out the unwritten rules.
- Control the bloodletting.
- Free the successor from restrictive commitments.
- Share your observations about people, but do not impose them.
- Let the successor's credentials speak for themselves; do not overpraise him or her.
- Plunge the newcomer in at the deep end.

Supply chain management
The business of managing the supply of goods and services that come into an organisation. There is little distinction to be made between supply chain management and LOGISTICS. Logistics refers to the strategic thinking behind the flow of materials; supply chain management is more concerned with the practical aspects of keeping that flow moving.

SWOT
A mnemonic for four key questions that any company needs to think about:

- Strengths. What are the company's strengths compared with those of its competitors?
- Weaknesses. What are the company's weaknesses compared with those of its competitors?
- Opportunities. What are the main opportunities for the company in its surrounding environment?

- Threats. What are the main threats to the company in its surrounding environment?

Some prefer to call it TOWS rather than SWOT, thereby placing greater emphasis on the questions about corporate environment than on those about the company itself.

SYNERGY
A modern philosopher's stone: the conceited belief of many managers that they can make two and two add up to five. A useful before-the-event justification for many otherwise unjustifiable TAKEOVERS. Synergy means that company A+B is worth more than company A and company B added together. There has always been something slightly smelly about the idea, because it seems to be applicable to any and every situation. If one manufacturer of sweets buys another manufacturer of sweets then synergy comes from the ECONOMIES OF SCALE that the two can make together. But if the manufacturer of sweets buys a paper company then synergy comes from using the paper in packaging the sweets. Anyone can make up any number of examples of this sort.

SYSTEM DYNAMICS
The study of systems (the way in which something organises its own internal procedures) as dynamic, constantly evolving entities. This requires sophisticated SIMULATION and computer modelling.

The concept has been applied to various aspects of business behaviour since the 1950s and has come to be widely used in the management of complex PROCESSES (such as petrochemicals plants and utilities). It is gradually being used by mainstream industry to help it to understand the impact of discrete events in a world where change is rapid, and where almost everything is interrelated.

Takeover

When one company obtains a majority of the shares in another. This can be achieved in two ways.

- As a friendly takeover, in which the company being taken over courts the takeover.
- As a hostile takeover, in which the company being taken over fights to prevent the predator from obtaining a majority of its shares.

There are many different types of defence that a company can adopt if it becomes the subject of a hostile takeover. Many of them have colourful names, such as the Pac-Man Defence, the Poison Pill and the Scorched Earth Defence.

In Anglo-Saxon economies, takeovers are fought as games in which both sides must follow fair rules. In the UK, the rules are laid down by the Takeover Panel, a group of respectable folk from the City of London. The guiding principles are that shareholders' interests come uppermost, and that all shareholders should be treated equally.

In continental Europe and Japan neither of these principles is widely respected. Different voting rights attaching to different categories of shares ensure that shareholders are never equal, least of all at the time of a potential takeover. The general shareholder's interest is often subsumed under that of a ruling coterie, family or financial institution. (See also MERGERS AND ACQUISITIONS.)

Tax shelter

A device (rather than a place) for sheltering income or capital from tax. The place to find tax shelters is a tax haven. Gifts to charity are a tax shelter, and so are accelerated depreciation schedules. So indeed are pension schemes, but here the shelter has a price: no access to the income for many years.

Frederick Winslow Taylor

The highly influential inventor of scientific management, a way of applying scientific methods to the art of management. Taylor was a talented man. He won the American doubles tennis championship in 1881 and he was a prolific inventor. He also created the PIECE-RATE system, and his ideas have had a profound influence on management thinkers since his death in 1915.

Scientific management was deeply rooted in the 19th century's obsession with science and scientific methods. All the foremen in Taylor's factories had stopwatches. The main criticism of Taylor's work is that it attempts to reduce human beings to little more than machines (and not very sophisticated ones at that).

TEASER

A short advertisement that precedes a series of bigger advertisements and titillates the audience for what is to come. Ironically, teasers do not normally mention the name of the product that they are designed to advertise. One of the most famous teasers was for R.J. Reynolds's Camel cigarettes. Launched in 1913, the teasers had slogans like "The Camels are Coming". No one in downtown Manhattan knew quite what to expect.

TECHNOLOGY TRANSFER

Most new technology is developed in the wealthy West. One way of spreading this around is for developing countries to demand, as a condition of a company winning any large contract, that it transfer some of its proprietary technology (patents, operating systems, designs, and so on) to the country granting the contract. This so-called technology transfer often occurs as part of large public-sector projects, or it is packaged as a form of government aid.

TELECOMMUTING

The practice whereby workers live and work in their suburban or rural homes and commute to their offices solely via the telephone, fax and computer MODEM. The potential of telecommuting has proved more limited than its promoters first thought. It is useful for people (like travelling salesmen) who can file written reports back to base without actually having to go there. Wider applications to whole workforces, in industries such as insurance, with corresponding savings in office overheads, have proved largely illusory. By and large, the value that workers obtain from companionship has been underestimated.

Test marketing

The MARKETING of a product or service in a limited geographic area to test the market's reactions before making a full launch. In test marketing the full panoply of marketing techniques are brought to bear on the product, but only in the limited area. So the television ADVERTISING campaign is only run on local TV, the press campaign in local newspapers, and so on.

Theory X and Y

One of the most famous theories about management behaviour. Expounded by Douglas McGregor, a social psychologist, who was professor of management at MIT for a decade from the mid-1950s, it claims that there are two fundamental styles of management: one is called Theory X, and one is called Theory Y.

Theory X is the traditional view of things. It assumes that humans have a natural aversion to work and will avoid it if they can. Therefore they have to be coerced and threatened to get them to do things. Managers who take this view generally get a hostile reaction from employees, which reinforces them in their view.

Theory Y, however, proposes that humans naturally find work satisfying, and that management systems built on that assumption will give individuals responsibility and freedom to attain a corporation's objectives under their own steam. McGregor argued that this Utopian style would produce far more VALUE than Theory X. Unfortunately, attempts to introduce it in anything like a pure form have proved largely unsuccessful.

Total quality management
The idea that quality is something that must be disseminated throughout an organisation, and not just left to a quality controller who examines goods as they emerge at the end of a production line (by which time it is too late to do much about them).

The European Foundation for Quality Management (EFQM) says that total quality management (TQM) is characterised by the following.

- The excellence of all managerial, operational and administrative processes.
- A culture of CONTINUOUS IMPROVEMENT in all aspects of the business.
- An understanding that quality improvement results in cost advantages and better PROFIT potential.
- The creation of more intensive relationships with customers and suppliers.
- The involvement of all personnel.
- Market-oriented organisational practices.

Total shareholder return
The total financial gain to a shareholder from an investment in a corporation over a period of time. The total shareholder return (TSR) is equal to the capital gain (the number of shares held by the shareholder times the increase in the company's share price over the period), plus the dividends paid out over the period, calculated on the assumption that those dividends are reinvested in the corporation by being used to buy more shares. TSR has become an important yardstick of the VALUE added by corporations over time.

TQM
See TOTAL QUALITY MANAGEMENT.

Trade barrier
Anything that discourages the free flow of trade. The most obvious barriers to trade are import duties (a percentage tax on imports) and quotas (a quantitative ceiling on the volume of imports). As

world trade organisations force more and more countries (often reluctantly) to dismantle these barriers, they erect a growing number of invisible barriers in their place. These include things like Byzantine distribution systems, which only locals can find their way around.

TRANSFER PRICING
A means of shifting a company's PROFIT from one country (with a high tax rate) to another (with a low tax rate). Transfer pricing skirts on the boundaries between tax avoidance (which is legal) and tax evasion (which is not). It usually involves a subsidiary (in country A) charging another subsidiary (in country B) a higher-than-market price for an intra-group purchase of goods or services. This makes no difference to the MULTINATIONAL'S overall PROFIT, but it shifts more of it to country B and less to country A, which is helpful if country B has a lower corporation tax rate than country A.

TROUBLESHOOTER
Sometimes known as an interim manager, a person sent into a company at a senior management level (and for a limited period of time) to sort out a particular problem. Troubleshooters are valued for the fresh eye that they can bring. Unlike MANAGEMENT CONSULTANTS, they go on to the company's payroll and they have a remit to do something about problems that they identify.

One description of an ideal troubleshooter from a firm that supplies them is as follows:

> *A troubleshooter, or crisis manager, is typically aged 40 or older, has at least ten years of board-level management experience and is able to gain a rapid insight into how a business works at all levels and across all functions, such as marketing, production and finance. He or she also needs to be a good communicator, creative and flexible, as well as mentally and physically tough enough to cope with the stresses of rescuing a company.*

True and fair
The Holy Grail for accountants who have to pledge that the set of figures they have checked or produced presents a true and fair view of a company's affairs. Accountants may believe that their brief is to be objective, but in many areas they are compelled to be subjective. One accountant's true and fair view may not be another's. There is thus no uniquely true and fair view of anything – not the market VALUE of Canary Wharf, nor the yield of an orange grove.

TSR
See TOTAL SHAREHOLDER RETURN.

Unique selling proposition
Commonly known as USP. The range of unique features that differentiate a product from its competitors and that can be conveyed to consumers in a simple ADVERTISING message. MARKETING departments, however, know that uniqueness is rare, and that it is too much to hope to find it in every new product. So uniqueness has given way to POSITIONING: the DIFFERENTIATION of a product from its competitors according to its position on a scale of qualities.

Value

The perceived worth of a product. Value depends on numerous factors, including quality, design and image, and it varies according to location. It is a subjective measure of what something is worth to its owner. This may be more than the price tag says it costs (as, say, in the case of jewellery with sentimental value); or it may be less (as in the case of a "free" airline ticket which demands that the traveller stay in a particular expensive hotel on arrival).

MARKETING can be seen as the art of making consumers feel that they have at least got value for money; that is, that the product (and all its associations) is worth to them at least as much as they paid for it.

Value is what buyers are willing to pay for, and superior value stems from offering lower prices than competitors for equivalent benefits, or providing unique benefits that more than offset a higher price.

Michael Porter

Value chain

A concept introduced by MICHAEL PORTER in his 1985 book *Competitive Advantage: Creating and Sustaining Superior Performance.* It is based on the idea that each firm in an industry can be seen as a chain of activities. Each link in the chain adds VALUE to the ultimate product or service. Companies can gain COMPETITIVE ADVANTAGE over others in one of two ways: by producing links in the value chain more cheaply, or by differentiating the links more desirably than their opponents.

Venture capital

Synonymous in most dictionaries with risk capital, venture capital is money for starting new companies or for building up young ones. It is subject to an unusually high degree of risk, and it expects most of its return to come from capital gain not dividends. Venture capital funds expect to find a few big winners and a large number of duds.

However, more so-called venture capital goes into the expansion of existing businesses or into the MANAGEMENT BUY-OUT of existing firms than goes into new businesses. And the amount of venture capital going into START-UPS in the United States, especially in high-tech industries, is generally higher than in Europe.

Vertical integration

The bringing together within one organisation of a number of different business operations that follow each other sequentially. For instance, if a company that makes cars buys the company that supplies it with headlamps, the car company is involved in backward vertical integration; if the car company buys a chain of car retailers it is engaged in forward vertical integration.

Vicious/virtuous circle

The idea that in business and economics it is possible to get into a sequence of events that almost inevitably leads on to something worse (a vicious circle) or something better (a virtuous circle). A company that is unexpectedly struck by a single disaster, for example, might find it the beginning of a vicious circle that leads on to the total collapse of its market. A widely publicised product defect might lead to a loss of consumer confidence. This, in turn, might lead to the undermining of its bankers' confidence in the company, which leads on to a shortage of WORKING CAPITAL. From there it is but a short step to cutting corners in manufacturing and to yet more product defects.

Virtual organisation

Virtual reality is the artificial creation of the sights, sounds and smells of reality itself, all of them experienced by wearing a sophisticated sort of headset. A virtual organisation has many of the characteristics of a real organisation, but it lacks the physical presence, the bits you can kick. It is an organisation that has OUTSOURCED most activity to others and has left for itself a small group of specialists who do a lot of electronic communicating.

VISION

Today considered to be a necessary part of any company's STRATEGY: an irrational, barrier-leaping ambition for the company. First find your vision, then devise a strategy to achieve it. (See also MISSION STATEMENT.)

A company vision ... must be crafted and articulated with clarity, continuity and consistency: clarity of expression that makes company objectives understandable and meaningful; continuity of purpose that underscores their enduring importance; and consistency of application across business units and geographical boundaries that ensures uniformity throughout the organisation.

Christopher Bartlett and Sumantra Ghoshal

Max Weber
A German professor of law and a social scientist who studied the nature of organisations. He was one of the first to attempt to classify different organisational types. In general, he divided them into three.

- The charismatic organisation, in which a single leader drives everybody on with his VISION and enthusiasm. This is the style of many religious organisations; it is also the style of the entrepreneurial young business.
- The traditional organisation, older and more stable, with an emphasis on traditional ways of doing things. Here accumulated culture is important. Large, well-established MULTINATIONALS fall into this category.
- The rational/legal organisation where everybody has a clearly designated role to play, and where there is a rigid rulebook. Such organisations include the military and companies modelled on it.

Website
A discrete location on the WORLD WIDE WEB containing a number of electronic pages with information about one particular subject or organisation (such as `www.economist.com`).

White goods/brown goods
Originally, white goods were household goods like sheets and towels. The expression has been taken over by MARKETING people to refer more specifically to white electrical household goods, such as refrigerators and washing machines. White goods can be contrasted with brown goods, an expression referring to electrical goods that were traditionally sold to consumers in brown casings, such as radios, televisions, record players, and so on. Now, of course, they are mostly sold in black casings, but they are still brown goods.

Window dressing
The universal practice of making published

accounts look as attractive as they can possibly (legally) be. The expression compares a company's accounts to a shop window in which everything is made to look as nice as possible and the torn bits are tied up and hidden from view. The real danger from window dressing is not so much that it will fool its audience (although this might matter depending on the circumstances), but that it will fool its authors, the company's managers. Many companies have hit the rocks because senior managers took their (slightly fantastical) accounts too literally.

Every set of published accounts is based on books which have been gently cooked or completely roasted. The figures which are fed twice a year to the investing public have all been changed to protect the guilty. It is the biggest con trick since the Trojan horse.

Ian Griffiths, *Creative Accounting*

WINDOW OF OPPORTUNITY

A tide in the affairs of corporations which, if taken at the flood, leads on to fortune. Businesses are seen as engines travelling along and looking in through passing windows. When the right window appears, action to enter it has to be taken immediately.

Many business opportunities depend crucially on timing. There are right times to take certain steps and wrong times. New products are only launched at certain seasons (not the week before Christmas, for example), and there are good and bad times for going to a stockmarket with a new issue. Miss a window of opportunity and, at best, you have to wait a while for the next one.

WORK-IN-PROGRESS

Referred to in the United States as work-in-process, this includes all the semi-finished goods and services in a business, things on their way from being raw materials to becoming finished products. Firms try to reduce expensive work-in-progress (WIP) to a minimum. For many companies, such as contractors, almost all their ASSETS consist of WIP. Valuing this unfinished business is significant in any estimation of such a company's worth.

WORKING CAPITAL
The difference between a company's current ASSETS and its current LIABILITIES; that is, the amount of cash it has free and available to use in the business. Current assets include easily sellable goods, cash and bank deposits. Current liabilities include debts due in less than one year, interest payments, and so on. The classic solution to a shortage of working capital is a visit to a bank.

WORLD WIDE WEB
Or www, the technology that enables people to use the INTERNET and to access the information on it no matter where they are coming from.

YIELD

In general, yield refers to the output of any of the FACTORS OF PRODUCTION (land, labour or capital). Thus yield can refer to the wheat produced per year per acre from a particular plot of land, or it can refer to the tonnes of coal dug up by a single miner in a year. It is most commonly used with reference to the annual return from an investment of capital. An investment of $1,000 that produces $90 in a year has a yield of 9%.

Specific sorts of yield include the following.

- The dividend yield. The annual pre-tax amount that shareholders receive as dividend, expressed as a percentage of the amount that they invested.
- The earnings yield. The pre-tax PROFIT of a company (its earnings) divided by the number of shares, expressed as a percentage of the price per share. This is the reciprocal of the P/E RATIO.
- The flat yield. The yield taking into account only the income earned on an investment; the sort of yield obtained from a bank deposit where the capital element does not change over time.
- Gross/net yield. The yield expressed before/after tax is paid.
- Redemption yield. A yield that takes into account any capital gain (or loss) to be made on the redemption of an investment. This is particularly useful in calculating the return to be made on fixed-interest securities (like government bonds). These are issued with a fixed rate of interest and then sold in the secondary market at a discount (or premium) to their redemption price. Whether it is a discount or a premium is determined by whether current market rates are higher or lower than the instrument's fixed rate.

ZERO-BASE BUDGETING

An important way of escaping from the bind of basing all annual BUDGETING on last year's figures, and then adding a fixed percentage to them. Zero-base budgeting involves justifying every budget item afresh every year.

Although this can strip away some unnecessary costs that have been blindly taken for granted, it can also take a lot of extra time, which, in many cases, is not justified by the saving. Zero-base budgeting is, however, useful as something that managers are aware might be employed should they become too slap-happy with more traditional budgeting methods.

ZERO-SUM GAME

A game in which for every winner there is an equal and opposite loser. The most common form of zero-sum game in business is the competition for MARKET SHARE. Some games (like roulette) are necessarily zero-sum games. What the players lose, the banker wins, and vice versa. Competing for market share is not necessarily a zero-sum game; it is so only if the size of the market is static. If new entrants increase the total market (as they might do by encouraging wider demand for the product in general), it can become a positive-sum game.

Part 3

APPENDICES

1 Abbreviations

AACSB	The International Association for Management Education
ABC	activity-based costing
AMBA	Association of MBA's
B2B	business-to-business
B2C	business-to-consumer
BCG	Boston Consulting Group
BPR	business process re-engineering
CPA	critical path analysis
CRM	customer relationship management
CSF	critical success factors
DCF	discounted cashflow
EFMD	European Foundation for Management Development
EMBA	executive MBA
EPS	earnings per share
EVA	economic value added
FMCG	fast-moving consumer goods
FIFO	first in, first out
FRN	floating rate note
GDP	gross domestic product
GMAT	Graduate Management Admissions Test
HRM	human resource management
IPO	initial public offering
IRR	internal rate of return
IT	information technology
JIT	just-in-time
KPI	key performance indicator
LAN	local area network
LIBOR	London Interbank Offered Rate
LIFO	last in, first out
M&A	mergers and acquisitions
MBA	Master's Degree in Business Administration
MBI	management buy-in
MBO	management buy-out
NPV	net present value
OEM	original equipment manufacture
OR	operational research
P/E ratio	price/earnings ratio
PMM	post-merger management

PPP	purchasing power parity
PR	public relations
R&D	research and development
SBU	strategic business unit
SEC	Securities and Exchange Commission
SME	small and medium-sized enterprises
TQM	total quality management
TSR	total shareholder return
USP	unique selling proposition
WIP	work-in-progress
WWW	World Wide Web

2 Selected business schools: North America

The Anderson School at UCLA
110 Westwood Plaza, Suite B 307
Los Angeles
CA 90025
US
Tel: +1 310 8256944
Fax: +1 310 8258582
E-mail: mba.admissions@anderson.ucla.edu
Website: www.anderson.ucla.edu

Arthur D. Little School of Management
194 Beacon Street
Chestnut Hill
MA 02467
US
Tel: +1 617 5522877
Fax: +1 617 5522051
E-mail: adlsom@adlittle.com
Website: www.adlsom.com

Carnegie Mellon University
Graduate School of Industrial Administration
500 Forbes Avenue
Pittsburgh
PA 15213-3890
US
Tel: +1 412 2682000
Fax: +1 412 2684209
E-mail: gsia-admissions@cmu.edu
Website: www.gsia.cmu.edu

University of Chicago
Graduate School of Business
1101 East 58th Street
Chicago
IL 60637
US
Tel: +1 773 7027369
Fax: +1 773 7029085
E-mail: admissions@gsb.chicago.edu
Website: www.gsb.uchicago.edu

Columbia Business School
Uris Hall
3022 Broadway
New York
NY 10027
US
Tel: +1 212 8541961
Fax: +1 212 6626754
E-mail: apply@claven.gsb.columbia.edu
Website: www.gsb.columbia.edu

Cornell University
Johnson Graduate School of Management
Sage Hall
Ithaca
NY 14853-6201
US
Tel: +1 607 2554526
Fax: +1 607 2550065
E-mail: mba@cornell.edu
Website: www.johnson.cornell.edu

Darden Graduate School of Business
Administration
University of Virginia
PO Box 6550
Charlottesville
VA 22906
US
Tel: +1 804 9247281
Fax: +1 804 2435033
E-mail: darden@virginia.edu
Website: www.darden.virginia.edu

Fuqua School of Business
Duke University
One Towerview Road
Durham
NC 27708
US
Tel: +1 919 6607705
Fax: +1 919 6818026
E-mail: fuqua-admissions@mail.duke.edu
Website: www.fuqua.duke.edu

Goizueta Business School
Emory University
1300 Clifton Road NE
Atlanta
GA 30322
US
Tel: +1 404 7276311
Fax: +1 404 7274612
E-mail: admissions@bus.emory.edu
Website: www.emory.edu/bus

Haas School of Business
University of California at Berkeley
440 Student Services Building
Berkeley
CA 94720-1902
US
Tel: +1 510 6421405
Fax: +1 510 6436659
E-mail: mbaadms@haas.berkeley.edu
Website: www.haas.berkeley.edu

Harvard Business School
Soldiers Field
Boston
MA 02163
US
Tel: +1 617 4956127
Fax: +1 617 4969272
E-mail: admissions@hbs.edu
Website: www.hbs.edu

Kellogg Graduate School of Management
Northwestern University
2001 Sheridan Road
Evanston
IL 60208-2001
US
Tel: +1 847 4913308
Fax: +1 847 4914960
E-mail: kellogg-admissions@nwu.edu
Website: www.kellogg.nwu.edu

McGill University
Faculty of Management
1001 Sherbrooke Street West, Suite 300
Montreal
Quebec, H3A 1G5
Canada
Tel: +1 514 3984066
Fax: +1 514 3982499
E-mail: mba@management.mcgill.ca
Website: www.management.mcgill.ca

University of Michigan Business School
701 Tappan Street
Ann Arbor
MI 48109-1234
US
Tel: +1 313 7635796
Fax: +1 313 7637804
E-mail: umbusmba@umich.edu
Website: www.bus.umich.edu

MIT Sloan School of Management
Massachusetts Institute of Technology
50 Memorial Drive
Cambridge
MA 02142
US
Tel: +1 617 2533730
Fax: +1 617 2536405
E-mail: mbaadmissions@sloan.mit.edu
Website: mitsloan.mit.edu/

Rotman School of Management
University of Toronto
105 St George Street
Toronto
Ontario, M5S 3E6
Canada
Tel: +1 416 9783499
Fax: +1 416 9785812
E-mail: mbaprog@mgmt.utoronto.ca
Website: www.mgmt.utoronto.ca

Stanford Graduate School of Business
Stanford University
Stanford
CA 94305-5015
US
Tel: +1 650 7232766
Fax: +1 650 7257831
E-mail: mbaapps@gsb.stanford.edu
Website: www-gsb.stanford.edu

Stern School of Business
New York University
44 West 4th Street
New York
NY 10012
US
Tel: +1 212 9980600
Fax: +1 212 9954231
E-mail: sternmba@stern.nyu.edu
Website: www.stern.nyu.edu

Thunderbird
The American Graduate School of International Management
15249 North 59th Avenue
Glendale
AZ 85306
US
Tel: +1 602 9787210
Fax: +1 602 4395432
E-mail: tbird@t-bird.edu
Website: www.t-bird.edu

Tuck School of Business Administration
Dartmouth College
100 Tuck Hall
Hanover
NH 03755
US
Tel: +1 603 6463162
Fax: +1 603 6461441
E-mail: tuck.admissions@dartmouth.edu
Website: www.tuck.dartmouth.edu

Warrington College of Business
University of Florida
134 Bryan Hall
PO Box 117152
Gainesville
FL 32611-7152
US
Tel: +1 352 3927992
Fax: +1 352 3928791
E-mail: floridamba@notes.cba.ufl.edu
Website: www.floridamba.ufl.edu

Wharton School
University of Pennsylvania
102 Vance Hall
3733 Spruce Street
Philadelphia
PA 19104-6361
US
Tel: +1 215 8986183
Fax: +1 215 8980120
E-mail: mba.admissions@wharton.upenn.edu
Website: www.wharton.upenn.ed

University of Wisconsin-Madison
Graduate School of Business
3150 Grainger Hall
975 University Avenue
Madison
WI 53706-1323
US
Tel: +1 608 2624000
Fax: +1 608 2654192
E-mail: uwmadmba@bus.wisc.edu
Website: www.wisc.edu/bschool/

Yale School of Management
135 Prospect Street
PO Box 208200
New Haven
CT 06520-8200
US
Tel: +1 203 4325932
Fax: +1 203 4327004
E-mail: mba.admissions@yale.edu
Website: mba.yale.edu

3 Selected business schools: UK

Ashridge
Berkhamsted
Hertfordshire HP4 1NS
UK
Tel: +44 1442 841143
Fax: +44 1442 841144
E-mail: info@ashridge.org.uk
Website: www.ashridge.org.uk

University of Bath School of Management
Claverton Down
Bath BA2 7AY
UK
Tel: +44 1225 323432/323341
Fax: +44 1225 82610
E-mail: mba-info@management.bath.ac.uk
Website:
www.bath.ac.uk/Departments/Management

University of Bradford Management Centre
Emm Lane
Bradford BD9 4JL
UK
Tel: +44 1274 234417
Fax: +44 1274 232311
E-mail: mba@bradford.ac.uk
Website: www.brad.ac.uk/acad/mancen

University of Cambridge
The Judge Institute of Management Studies
Trumpington Street
Cambridge CB2 1AG
UK
Tel: +44 1223 337051/2/3
Fax: +44 1223 339581
E-mail: mba-enquiries@jims.cam.ac.uk
Website: www.jims.cam.ac.uk/programmes.html

City University Business School
Frobisher Crescent
Barbican Centre
London EC2Y 8HB
UK
Tel: +44 20 7477 8607/8
Fax: +44 20 7477 8898
E-mail: cubs-postgrad@city.ac.uk
Website: www.business.city.ac.uk

Cranfield School of Management
Cranfield
Bedford MK43 0AL
UK
Tel: +44 1234 754431
Fax: +44 1234 752439
E-mail: p.hayes@cranfield.ac.uk
Website: www.cranfield.ac.uk/som/mba

University of Durham Business School
Mill Hill Lane
Durham DH1 3LB
UK
Tel: +44 191 3742233
Fax: +44 191 3741230
E-mail: pg.bus@durham.ac.uk
Website: www.dur.ac.uk/udbs/

University of Edinburgh Business School
7 Bristo Square
Edinburgh EH8 9AL
UK
Tel: +44 131 6508066
Fax: +44 131 6508077
E-mail: management.school@ed.ac.uk
Website: www.ems.ed.ac.uk

University of Glasgow Business School
University of Glasgow
Glasgow G12 8QQ
UK
Tel: +44 141 3303993
Fax: +44 141 3304939
E-mail: m.b.a.admissions@mgt.gla.ac.uk
Website: www.gla.ac.uk/schools/business

Henley Management College
Greenlands
Henley-on-Thames
Oxon RG9 3AU
UK
Tel: +44 1491 418803
Fax: +44 1491 418899
E-mail: mba@henleymc.ac.uk
Website: www.henleymc.ac.uk/mba

Imperial College Management School
53 Prince's Gate
Exhibition Road
London SW7 2PG
UK
Tel: +44 20 7594 9205
Fax: +44 20 7823 7685
E-mail: ftmba.mschool@ic.ac.uk
Website: www.ms.ic.ac.uk

Lancaster University Management School
The MBA Office
Lancaster University
Management School
Lancaster LA1 4YX
UK
Tel: +44 1524 594068
Fax: +44 1524 592417
E-mail: mba@lancaster.ac.uk
Website: www.lums.lancs.ac.uk/mba/

London Business School
Regent's Park
London NW1 4SA
UK
Tel: +44 20 7706 6859
Fax: +44 20 7724 7875
E-mail: mbainfo@london.edu
Website: www.london.edu

Manchester Business School
Booth Street West
Manchester M15 6PB
UK
Tel: +44 161 2756530
Fax: +44 161 2756556
E-mail: admissions@fs2.mbs.ac.uk
Website: www.mbs.ac.uk

University of Nottingham
Business School
Jubilee Campus
Wollaton Road
Nottingham NG8 1BB
UK
Tel: +44 115 9515500
Fax: +44 115 9515503
E-mail: MBA@nottingham.ac.uk
Website: www.nottingham.ac.uk/unbs

The Open University Business School
Walton Hall
Milton Keynes MK7 6AA
UK
Tel: +44 8700 100311 (UK)
+322 644 3372 (Brussels)
Fax: +44 1908 654320
E-mail: oubs-ilgen@open.ac.uk
Website: oubs.open.ac.uk

University of Oxford
Said Business School
The Radcliffe Infirmary
Woodstock Road
Oxford OX2 6HE
UK
Tel: +44 1865 224371
Fax: +44 1865 228471
E-mail: enquiries@sbs.ox.ac.uk
Website: www.sbs.ox.ac.uk

Sheffield University Management School
9 Mappin Street
Sheffield S1 4DT
UK
Tel: +44 114 2223378
Fax: +44 114 2223348
E-mail: sums@sheffield.ac.uk
Website: www.sums.ac.uk/mba

University of Stirling
Faculty of Management
Stirling FK9 4LA
UK
Tel: +44 1786 467415
Fax: +44 1786 450776
E-mail: mba@stir.ac.uk
Website: www.stir.ac.uk/mba

University of Strathclyde
Graduate School of Business
199 Cathedral Street
Glasgow G4 0QU
UK
Tel: +44 141 5536118/9
Fax: +44 141 5528851
E-mail: admissions@gbs.strath.ac.uk
Website: www.worldclassmba.com

Warwick Business School
University of Warwick
Coventry CV4 7AL
UK
Tel: +44 24 7652 3922
Fax: +44 24 7652 4643
E-mail: fmbain@wbs.warwick.ac.uk
Website: www.wbs.warwick.ac.uk/mba/

4 Selected business schools: Europe

SDA Bocconi
Masters Division
Via Balilla 16–18
20136 Milan
Italy
Tel: +39 2 58363281
Fax: +39 2 58363725
E-mail: MD@sda.uni-bocconi.it
Website: www.sda.uni-bocconi.it

University of Dublin – Trinity College
School of Business Studies
University of Dublin
Trinity College
Dublin 2
Ireland
Tel: +353 1 6081024
Fax: +353 1 6799503
E-mail: TrinityMBA@tcd.ie
Website: www.tcd.ie/Business_Studies/MBA/

ESADE
Avenida de Pedralbes 60-62
08034 Barcelona
Spain
Tel: +34 93 2802995
Fax: +34 93 4952077
E-mail: info@esade.es
Website: www.esade.es

ESCP-EAP Graduate School of Management
6 avenue de la Porte de Champerret
75838 Paris Cedex 17
France
Tel: +33 1 4409 3331/32
Fax: +33 1 4409 3335
E-mail: mba@escp-eap.net
Website: www.escp-eap.net

HEC Paris Graduate Business School
1 rue de la Libération
78351 Jouy-en-Josas Cedex
France
Tel: +33 1 3967 7374
Fax: +33 1 3967 7465
E-mail: isadmission@hec.fr
Website: www.mba.hec.fr

Helsinki School of Economics and Business Administration
Runeberginkatu 14-16
00100 Helsinki
Finland
Tel: +358 9 4313 8224
Fax: +358 9 4313 8613
E-mail: mbafi@hkkk.fi
Website: www.hkkk.fi/mbafi

IE – Instituto de Empresa
María de Molina 13
28006 Madrid
Spain
Tel: +34 91 5689610
Fax: +34 91 4115503
E-mail: admissions@ie.edu
Website: www.ie.edu

IESE – International Graduate School of Management
University of Navarra
Avenida Pearson 21
08034 Barcelona
Spain
Tel: +34 93 2534229
Fax: +34 93 2534343
E-mail: mbainfo@iese.edu
Website: www.iese.edu

IMD – International Institute for Management Development
Chemin de Bellerive 23
PO Box 915
1001 Lausanne
Switzerland
Tel: +41 21 6180298
Fax: +41 21 6180615
E-mail: mbainfo@imd.ch
Website: www.imd.ch

INSEAD
Boulevard de Constance
77305 Fontainebleau Cedex
France
Tel: +33 1 6072 4005
Fax: +33 1 6074 5530
E-mail: mba.info@insead.fr
Website: www.insead.fr/mba

E.M. Lyon
23 avenue Guy de Collongue
BP 174, 69132 Ecully Cedex
France
Tel: +33 4 7833 7865
Fax: +33 4 7833 6165
E-mail: cesmamba@em-lyon.com
Website: www.em-lyon.com

Maastricht School of Management
PO Box 1203
6201 BE Maastricht
Netherlands
Tel: +31 43 3870808
Fax: +31 43 3870800
E-mail: information@msm.nl
Website: www.msm.nl

Norwegian School of Management
Postboks 9386 Gronland
0135 Oslo
Norway
Tel: +47 2257 6200
Fax: +47 2257 6282
E-mail: graduate@bi.no
Website: www.bi.no/graduate

Universiteit Nyenrode
The Netherlands Business School
Straatweg 25
3621 BG Breukelen
The Netherlands
Tel: +31 346 291607
Fax: +31 346 250595
E-mail: mba@nyenrode.nl
Website: www.nyenrode.nl

Rotterdam School of Management
Erasmus Graduate School of Business
PO Box 1738
3000 DR Rotterdam
The Netherlands
Tel: +31 10 4082222
Fax: +31 10 4529509
E-mail: rsm@rsm.nl
Website: www.rsm.nl

The Michael Smurfit Graduate School of Business
University College Dublin
Carysfort Avenue
Blackrock
Co Dublin
Ireland
Tel: +353 1 7068860
Fax: +353 1 2831911
E-mail: padmin@ucd.ie
Website: www.ucd.ie/gsb

Solvay Business School
Université Libre de Bruxelles
21 Avenue F.D. Roosevelt
CP-145/01
1050 Brussels
Belgium
Tel: +32 2 6504167
Fax: +32 2 6504199
E-mail: mba@ulb.ac.be
Website: www.ulb.ac.be/soco/solvay/mba/

Theseus International Management Institute
BP 169, rue Albert Einstein
06903 Sophia Antipolis Cedex
France
Tel: +33 4 9294 5100
Fax: +33 4 9365 3837
E-mail: admissions@theseus.fr
Website: www.theseus.edu

5 Selected business schools: the rest of the world

Asian Institute of Management
McMicking Campus
123 Paseo de Roxas
1260 Makati City
Philippines
Tel: +63 2 8924011-25
Fax: +63 2 8934595
E-mail: admissions@aim.edu.ph
Website: www.aim.edu.ph

Australian Graduate School of Management
University of New South Wales and
University of Sydney
Sydney
NSW 2052
Australia
Tel: +61 2 9931 9225
Fax: +61 2 9931 9231
E-mail: chrisk@agsm.edu.au
Website: www.agsm.edu.au

University of Cape Town
Graduate School of Business
Private Bag Rondebosch
7701 Cape Town
South Africa
Tel: +27 21 4061338/9
Fax: +27 21 4215693
E-mail: mbaenqry@gsb2.uct.ac.za
Website: www.gsb.uct.ac.za

University of Hong Kong
School of Business
Room 733, 7th floor
Meng Wah Complex
Hong Kong
Tel: +852 2859 1021
Fax: +852 2858 5614
E-mail: hkumba@business.hku.hk
Website: www.business.hku.hk

Hong Kong University of Science and Technology
School of Business and Management
Clearwater Bay
Kowloon
Hong Kong
Tel: +852 2358 7539/7544
Fax: +852 2705 9596
E-mail: mba@ust.hk
Website: www.bm.ust.hk/~mba

Indian Institute of Management
Vastrapur
380015 Ahmedabad
Gujarat
India
Tel: +91 79 6307241 ext. 4633
Fax: +91 79 6306896/6300352
E-mail: admission@adminlan.iimahd.ernet.in
Website: www.iimahd.ernet.in

Macquarie Graduate School of Management
Macquarie University
NSW 2109
Australia
Tel: +61 2 98509017
Fax: +61 2 98509022
E-mail: gsminfo@gsm.mq.edu.au
Website: www.gsm.mq.edu.au

Melbourne Business School
University of Melbourne
200 Leicester Street
Carlton
Victoria 3053
Australia
Tel: +61 3 9349 8100
Fax: +61 3 9349 8133
E-mail: a.sankey@mbs.unimelb.edu.au
Website: www.mbs.unimelb.edu.au

University of Otago
Graduate School of Business
PO Box 56
Dunedin
New Zealand
Tel: +64 3 4798046
Fax: +64 3 4798045
E-mail: mbainfo@commerce.otago.ac.nz
Website: www.otago.ac.nz/mba

National University of Singapore
Graduate School of Business
10 Kent Ridge Crescent
119260 Singapore
Tel: +65 8742068
Fax: +65 7782681
E-mail: gsbadm1@nus.edu.sg
Website:
www.fba.nus.edu.sg/postgrad/gsb/index.htm

Wits Business School
University of the Witwatersrand
PO Box 98
2050 Wits
South Africa
Tel: +27 11 4885600
Fax: +27 11 6432336
E-mail: reg@zeus.mgmt.wits.ac.za
Website: sunsite.wits.ac.za/wbs

6 Sources of information on MBAs

AACSB – The International Association for
Management Education
600 Emerson Road, Suite 300
St Louis, MO 63141-6762
US
Tel: +1 314 8728481
Fax: +1 314 8728495
Website: www.aacsb.edu

Association of MBAs
15 Duncan Terrace
London N1 8BZ
UK
Tel: +44 20 7837 3375
Fax: +44 20 7278 3634
Website: www.mba.org.uk

European Foundation of Management
Development (EFMD)
Rue Gachard 88
1050 Brussels
Belgium
Tel: +32 2 6290810
Fax: +32 2 6290811
E-mail: info@efmd.be
Website: www.efmd.be

7 20 major management consultants

Andersen Consulting
Arthur Andersen
Bain & Co
Roland Berger & Partner
Booz-Allen & Hamilton
Boston Consulting Group
Cap Gemini
CSC
Deloitte Consulting
Ernst & Young
IBM Consulting
A.T. Kearney
KPMG
Arthur D. Little
McKinsey & Company
Mercer Consulting Group
Monitor Company
PA Consulting Group
PricewaterhouseCoopers
Towers Perrin

8 Sources of business information

DIRECTORIES

Asia's 7,500 largest companies, ELC International, UK.

Bankers' Almanac, Reed Information Services, UK.
Contact information for central, commercial, merchant and savings banks worldwide.

CIA World Factbook
Provides current profiles on over 250 countries, including social, economic and constitutional information.

Crawford's Directory of City Connections 2000, AP Information Services, UK.

Directory of Directories, Gale Research.
A predominantly American list of directories on many topics, including business and finance.

Directory of Directors, Bowker-Saur, UK.
Information on UK companies' financial and public relations advisers.

Directory of International Sources of Business Information, Pitman, UK.

Europe's 15,000 largest companies, ELC International, UK.

Hoover's Handbook, Hoover's Business Press, US.
Profiles of over 750 major American companies.

International Directory of Business Information Sources & Services, Europa, UK.

Japan Company Handbook, Toyo Keizai, Japan.
Details on all Japan's publicly traded companies.

Key British Enterprises, Dun & Bradstreet, UK and US.

Major Companies of Europe, Graham & Whiteside, UK.

Major Companies of the Arab World, Graham & Whiteside, UK.

Major Companies of the Far East & Australia, Graham & Whiteside, UK.

Principal International Businesses, Dun & Bradstreet, UK and US.

Sources of Comparative International Statistics, CBD Publishing, UK.
Sources of European Economic Information, Gower, UK.
The Economist Intelligence Unit, Country Reporting Service, EIU, UK.
Quarterly profiles of over 180 countries with political and economic comment and statistics.
The Times 1000, Times Books, UK.
Annual ranking of the largest publicly traded companies in major markets worldwide.
Who Owns Whom: Australasia & the Far East, Dun & Bradstreet, UK and US.
Who Owns Whom: Continental Europe, Dun & Bradstreet, UK and US.
Who Owns Whom: North America, Dun & Bradstreet, UK and US.
Who Owns Whom: United Kingdom & Northern Ireland, Dun & Bradstreet, UK and US.

SELECTED ELECTRONIC SERVICES AND DATABASES

Services

Bloomberg
Real-time news and statistical information on equities, bonds and commodities for major markets worldwide.

Reuters
Real-time news, statistical information and trading systems for major markets worldwide.

Primark Datastream
Historical statistical information for the world's major equity, bond and commodities markets, plus economic country data.

FT Profile
Full-text of the *Financial Times*, *The Economist*, global coverage of magazines and newspapers, company information and market research reports.

Reuters Business Briefing
Business news from over 2,000 sources worldwide.

Dialog Corporation
Dialog, DataStar and Profound online hosts; over 1,000 global sources of business, scientific and general information, as well as market and investment analysts' research.

Lexis-Nexis
Business, government and legal information for the US and EU member countries.

Dow Jones Interactive
Full-text of *The Wall Street Journal*, *Barron's* and a range of news wires and publications.

Nikkei Telecom/Japan News & Retrieval Service
News and data on Japanese business and finance.

Databases

ABI/Inform Global (Host: Dialog)
Articles from over 1,000 business and management journals available back to 1971.

Kompass (Host: Dialog)
Also available on CD-ROM. Regularly updated details on companies in Africa, Middle East, North America, Asia/Pacific and Europe.

Dun's Market Identifiers (Hosts: Dialog; Profound)
Credit reports on millions of US private companies.

Harvard Business Review (Hosts: Dialog; Lexis-Nexis)
Full text or summaries of every article appearing in the HBR since 1971.

Management Contents (Hosts: Dialog; Datastar)
Summaries of articles from hundreds of business and legal publications.

Standard & Poor's Register (Host: Dialog)
Biographical details of all American senior managers.

Textline (Hosts: FT Profile; Lexis-Nexis)
Full-text information and digests from over 1,000 international publications.

9 Useful websites

Here are some websites taken from *Pocket Internet* recommended by those who work for or read *The Economist*.

BUSINESS

`adage.com`
The *Advertising Age*, a worldwide marketing and advertising industry newspaper

`cbs.marketwatch.com`
Rich source of market and economic news for investors from the CBS stable

`mckinseyquarterly.com/home.htm`
Library of articles and research from the management consultancy McKinsey

`strategis.ic.gc.ca`
Canadian business information site, featuring company directories, trade and investment resources and economic analysis

`www.acca-usa.org`
Association of Chartered Certified Accountants site, listing many accounting resources

`www.accountingweb.co.uk`
British accountants' community

`www.bnet.co.uk`
A source of practical management information for British businesses

`www.businessmonitor.co.uk`
A collection of professional business advisers' knowledge and expertise. Monitors the legislative and regulatory framework affecting business and investment in the UK, Europe, North America, South-East Asia, China, Africa, Middle East and major offshore centres, providing a useful free resource to organisations wishing to expand their businesses into new markets

`www.carol.co.uk`
Company annual reports and other investor information

`www.ceoexpress.com`
Huge list of well-organised links to key business, Internet, media, finance and many other resources

www.e-business.pwcglobal.com
PricewaterhouseCoopers' e-business site
www.eiu.com
Global business information and analysis from the Economist Intelligence Unit, part of The Economist Group
www.euro-emu.co.uk
Emunet, a resource devoted to Europe's single currency
www.ft.com
The *Financial Times*, an excellent source for international business news
www.gbn.org
Home of the Global Business Network, with a forum for members' exchanges
www.globalsources.com
Product and trade information and links for volume buyers of consumer, business and industrial goods
www.guru.com
Network for professionals and independent contractors
www.hoovers.com
Global company directory with financial data, company news and links
www.iisg.nl/~w3vl
The World Wide Web Virtual Library's guide to the history of labour and business
www.oanda.com
Olsen and Associates' currency resource, including forecasts, historical tables and converters
www.propertymall.co.uk
News and property information for the commercial-property industry in Britain
www.smartmoney.com
The *Wall Street Journal*'s magazine of personal business, including a customisable portfolio tracker
www.strategy-business.com
Community site for business leaders encouraging the exchange of new business ideas, including articles and book reviews
www.thebiz.co.uk
Business directory and database with a strong British focus

www.thomasregister.com
Searchable database of brand names, products and services from the Thomas Register of American manufacturers
www.ukindustry.co.uk/ukidir.htm
A directory of British companies categorised by industry
www.virginbiz.net
Portal for small businesses, with strategies for starting a dot.com company
www.wsj.com
The *Wall Street Journal*'s Europe, US and Asia editions available on a subscription basis

EMPLOYMENT
careers.wsj.com
The *Wall Street Journal*'s careers section
jobasia.com
Large Asian recruitment website
www.adecco.com
Job-finding site from one of the world's largest recruitment companies
www.adecco.co.uk
British branch of adecco.com
www.cityjobs.co.uk
Well-organised site for job postings in Britain
www.cofinders.com
Helps start-ups to find partners
www.emdsnet.com
Global recruitment services from EMDS, an international consultancy
www.latpro.com
Latin American professional recruitment website, for Spanish and Portuguese speakers
www.pianetalavoro.ch
Recruitment site for jobs in Switzerland and northern Italy
www.referencenow.com
Meeting place for job applicants and employers
www.vaultreports.com
Careers information and employment research site
www.workoplis.com
Canadian careers site

www.workunlimited.co.uk
Careers website from the *Guardian*, a British newspaper

FINANCE

www.bloomberg.com
Financial market updates and analysis from Bloomberg
www.ebrd.com
The European Bank for Reconstruction and Development, which invests in Eastern Europe
www.fiafii.org/default.asp
The Futures Industry Association
www.globalfindata.com
Current and historical financial data
www.hedgeindex.com
Statistical database on hedge fund performance
www.ifc.org
The International Finance Corporation
www.marhedge.com
News bulletins and information on hedge funds
www.napf.co.uk
The UK's National Association of Pension Funds, representing the occupational pensions movement
www.reuters.com
Financial updates from Reuters
www.sec.gov
The Securities and Exchange Commission
www.stockcharts.com
Free stock charting, market analysis and financial tools
www.thestreet.com
Detailed reports and analysis from Wall Street

SEARCH ENGINES

search.netscape.com
Netscape
www.alltheweb.com
Fast search
www.altavista.com
AltaVista
www.askjeeves.com
Question and answer service

`www.deja.com`
DejaNews (newsgroup search engine)
`www.excite.com`
Excite
`www.google.com`
Google
`www.lycos.com`
Lycos
`www.northernlight.com`
Northern Light
`www.yahoo.com`
Yahoo

10 Recommended reading

Adams, Scott, *The Dilbert Principle*, HarperCollins, 1996.

Ansoff, Igor, *Corporate Strategy*, McGraw-Hill, 1965.

— *Strategic Management*, Macmillan, 1979.

— *Implanting Strategic Management*, Prentice-Hall, 1984.

Argyris, Chris, *Personality and Organisation*, Harper and Row, 1957.

— *Organisational Learning: A Theory of Action Perspective* (with Donald Schon), Addison-Wesley, 1978.

Barnard, Chester I., *The Functions of the Executive*, Harvard University Press, 1938 and 1968.

Bennis, Warren, *Organisation Development: Its Nature, Origins and Prospects*, Addison-Wesley, 1969.

Bennis, Warren and Nanus, Burt, *Leaders*, Harper and Row, 1985.

Bennis, Warren and Townsend, Robert, *Reinventing Leadership*, Piatkus, 1995.

Blanchard, Kenneth and Johnson, Spencer, *The One Minute Manager*, William Morrow, 1992.

De Bono, Edward, *Lateral Thinking for Management*, McGraw-Hill, 1971.

— *I am Right, You are Wrong*, Viking, 1990.

Brealey, Richard and Myers, Stewart, *Principles of Corporate Finance*, 5th edition, McGraw-Hill, 1996.

Chandler, Alfred D., *Strategy and Structure*, MIT Press, 1962.

Christensen, C., *The Innovator's Dilemma*, Harvard Business School Press, 1997.

Collins, J. and Porras, J., *Built to Last*, HarperBusiness, 1994.

Coupland, Douglas, *Microserfs*, HarperCollins, 1995.

Crosby, P.B., *Quality is Free*, McGraw-Hill, 1979.

Deming, W. Edwards, *Out of the Crisis*, MIT Press, 1986.

Downes, Larry and Mui, Chunka, *Unleashing the Killer App*, Harvard Business School Press, 1998.
Drucker, Peter, *The Practice of Management*, Harper and Row, 1954.
— *Age of Discontinuity*, Macmillan, 1969.
— *Managing in Turbulent Times*, Harper and Row, 1980.
— *Innovation and Entrepreneurship*, Harper and Row, 1985.
— *Managing for the Future*, Butterworth Heinemann, 1993.
Fayol, Henri, *Administration Industrielle et Générale*, 1916; English translation, Pitman, 1949.
Follett, Mary Parker, *Group Organisation*, Longmans, 1918.
— *Creative Experience*, Longmans, 1924.
Gilbreth, Frank, *Motion Study*, Van Nostrand, 1911.
Gilbreth, Frank and Gilbreth, Lilian, *The Psychology of Management*, Sturgis and Walton, 1914.
Hamel, Gary and Prahalad, C.K., *Competing for the Future*, Harvard Business School Press, 1994.
Hammer, Michael and Champy, James, *Re-engineering the Corporation*, HarperBusiness, 1993.
Handy, Charles, *The Age of Unreason*, Business Books, 1989.
— *Understanding Organisations*, 4th edition, Penguin, 1993.
Herzberg, Frederick, *The Motivation to Work*, John Wiley, 1959.
— *Managerial Choice – To be Efficient and to be Human*, Dow Jones, 1976.
Hindle, Tim, *Guide to Management Ideas*, Profile Books, 2000.
Hofstede, Geert, *Cultures and Organisations: Software of the Mind*, McGraw Hill, 1991.
Iacocco, Lee, *Iacocco: An Autobiography*, Bantam Books, 1984.
Jay, Anthony, *Management and Machiavelli*, Hodder & Stoughton, 1967.

Juran, J.J. and Gryna, F.M., *Quality Control Handbook*, McGraw-Hill, 1988.
Kanter, Rosabeth Moss, *Men and Women of the Corporation*, Basic Books, 1977.
— *The Change Masters*, Simon and Schuster, 1983.
— *When Giants Learn to Dance*, Simon and Schuster, 1989.
Kaplan, Robert, and Norton, David, *The Balanced Scorecard: Translating Strategy into Action*, Harvard Business School Press, 1996.
Keller, Kevin Lane, *Strategic Brand Management*, Prentice-Hall, 1998.
Kotler, Philip, *Marketing Management*, Millennium edition, Prentice-Hall, 1999.
Kotter, John, *The Leadership Factor*, The Free Press, 1988.
Levitt, Theodore, *The Marketing Mode*, McGraw-Hill, 1969.
— *The Marketing Imagination*, The Free Press, 1983.
Lewin, Kurt, *Resolving Social Conflicts*, Harper and Row, 1948.
Lewis, Michael, *Liar's Poker*, Hodder & Stoughton, 1989.
Likert, Rensis, *New Patterns of Management*, McGraw-Hill, 1961.
— *The Human Organisation: Its Management and Value*, McGraw-Hill, 1967.
Maslow, Abraham, *Motivation and Personality*, Harper and Row, 1954.
Mayo, Elton, *The Human Problems of an Industrial Civilisation*, Harvard Business School Press, 1933.
McClelland, P., *Motivating Economic Achievement*, The Free Press, 1969.
McGregor, Douglas, *The Human Side of the Enterprise*, McGraw-Hill, 1960.
Mintzberg, Henry, *The Nature of Managerial Work*, Harper and Row, 1973.
— *The Structuring of Organisations*, Prentice-Hall, 1979.
— *Mintzberg on Management*, The Free Press, 1989.

Morton, Michael Scott, *The Corporation of the 1990s*, Oxford University Press, 1991.
Ohmae, Kenichi, *Triad Power, The Coming Shape of Global Competition*, The Free Press, 1985.
— *The Borderless World*, HarperBusiness, 1990.
Ostroff, F., *The Horizontal Organisation*, Oxford University Press, 1999.
Parkinson, C. Northcote, *Parkinson's Law or the Pursuit of Progress,* Penguin, 1957.
Peter, Laurence J. and Hull, Raymond, *The Peter Principle,* William Morrow, 1968.
Peters, Tom and Waterman, Robert, *In Search of Excellence,* Harper and Row, 1982.
Peters, Tom, *Thriving on Chaos*, Alfred A. Knopf, 1987.
Pine, B.J., *Mass Customisation: the New Frontier in Business Competition*, Harvard Business School Press, 1999.
Porter, Michael, *Competitive Strategy: Techniques for Analysing Industries and Competitors,* The Free Press, 1980.
— *Competitive Advantage: Creating and Sustaining Superior Performance,* The Free Press, 1985.
Schein, Edgar, *Organisational Psychology,* Prentice-Hall, 1980.
Schumacher, E.F., *Small is Beautiful,* Briggs, 1973.
Schwartz, Peter, *The Art of the Long View,* John Wiley, 1996.
Senge, Peter, *The Fifth Discipline,* Doubleday, 1990.
Sloan, A.P., *My Years with General Motors,* Doubleday, 1954.
Taylor, Frederick, *A Piece Rate System*, McGraw-Hill, 1895 (republished 1985).
— *Shop Management*, Harper, 1903.
— *The Principles of Scientific Management,* Harper, 1911.
Townsend, Robert, *Up the Organisation,* Michael Joseph, 1970.
Urwick, Lyndall F., *The Elements of Administration,* Harper and Bros, 1944.

Velasquez, M.G., *Business Ethics: Concepts and Cases*, Prentice-Hall, 1992.
Waterman, Robert, *The Renewal Factor*, Bantam, 1987.
Weber, Max, *The Theory of Social and Economic Organisation*, The Free Press, 1947.